To: Jer

MW01122335

Sammy "G"

1/24/21

The Untold Story of
My Father

Jerry,
Thanks for coming out
Great to see you.
Blair T. Kenny

By
Gina Gingello
Blair T. Kenny

Sammy "G"

The Untold Story
of My Father

By
Gina Gingello
Blair T. Kenny

2nd edition

ISBN: 978-0-578-86568-3

FOREWARD

This book is the story of the life of Rochester Mafia Boss, Salvatore "Sammy G" Gingello, as told by his daughter Gina Gingello. It is also the story of Gina's life and the special relationship she shared with her father. The book is both a "Love Story" and a "Tragedy."

It is a composite of family photos, Gina's personal recollections, and my own research into Sammy G's life. Stories told by Gina are interwoven with newspaper articles of Sam's arrests, which I have used as a time reference, to place Gina's memories in perspective.

Although the information is mixed together it will be easy to differentiate between when Gina is speaking and when I am describing a news event. Gina always refers to Sam as "dad" "daddy" or "my father", and she speaks in the first person. When I have added information to the sequence of events I always refer to Sam either by name or his nickname, "Sammy G." More times than not my information will be accompanied by a newspaper article.

The book begins with the Gingello family history and then delves into Gina's Love Story about her relationship with, and memories of, her father. It ends in tragedy as Gina describes the aftermath of growing up without him. Gina was only 14 years old when Salvatore "Sammy G" Gingello was murdered on April 23, 1978.

For Gina it was way too much to handle. For her, time stopped on that day. She would be "Forever 14."

Blair T. Kenny

Dedications:

First and foremost, to my father: For the eternal love he has given me even after his death. The beautiful memories which I will always cherish and was able to share with everyone.

To Rocky and my four amazing children; Angelo, Nico, Santina, and Christina: For being there for me throughout my bouts of depression and times when I did not want to get out of bed, but they made me and kept me on my toes.

To my seven beautiful grandchildren; Gianni, Guliana, Alexandria, Luca, Giovanni, and Nick: They have made my family complete. God willing, He will bless Rocky and I with more grandchildren.

To Tom Marotta: For sticking by my father, my family and myself, since the age of 13. Tom has always been there for all of the Gingello family, especially my children and grandchildren, no matter what.

Tom Marotta and Gina Gingello,
Summer of 2020.

"THE WAYS ARE MANY..."

Gina Gingello

Left to right are Gina, Nico, Santina, Christina, Angelo, and Rocco.

Table Of Contents

Introduction

When I was 14 years old, Mr. Tuttle, a newspaper reporter from the Democrat and Chronicle, gave me the opportunity to write a love letter concerning my father. At that time it got picked up by the Associated Press, and then circulated around the country. He told me then that when I got older I should write another love letter. Thanks to Blair Kenny taking on my project, I was able to do just that in the form of this book. Blair has been able to help bring me some degree of closure after all these years.

This book is about the ups and downs of my life growing up without my father. It is about the people I have come in contact with and spoken to concerning my father's death. This book is about the milestones in my life and my childrens' lives that my father was not here to share in. This book is about the sadness that I have kept locked up inside me for the last 42 years.

Gina Gingello

Chapter One:

The Giglio (Gigillo) Family Comes to America
1922

In early **January of 1922,** Antonio Gigillo, along with his wife Gaetana and their five children, left Italy and came to America, like thousands of Italian immigrants before them, making the long journey across the Atlantic Ocean before arriving at Ellis Island in New York.

The family eventually settled into a home in Rochester, N.Y. at 148 Davis St. On **Jan. 31, 1922,** Antonio received his Certificate of Naturalization issued by the Department of Labor.

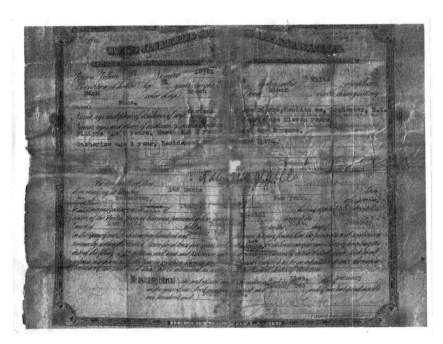

1922 Certificate of Naturalization for Antonio Gigillo, his wife Gaetana, and their five children.

From the signature on The Certificate of Naturalization document, the Gingello family name appears to originally have been "Gigillo" although the typed version of the name clearly says Antonio "Giglio." At some point the family name was changed to Gingello.

The Certificate of Naturalization issued by the Department of Labor on **Jan. 31, 1922** listed Anthony Giglio (Gigillo), his wife Gaetana and their five children by name and age. Details included on this document were **Description of holder**: Anthony Giglio (Gigillo), 31 years old, 4 feet 11 and 1/2 inches tall; White, dark complexion, brown eyes and black hair; **Wife:** Gaetana, age 26; **Children**: James, age 11; Filippa, age 9; Nardo, age 7; Michael, age 2; Catherine, age 1.

The red dot (bottom left) is **148 Davis St.** The map shows the location of the **Gigillo family home and its proximity to the Public Market.**

James Giglio (Gigillo), age 11 in 1922, was Salvatore "Sammy G" Gingello's father. At some point the family changed their last name to Gingello.

As stated in the document, the family settled in Rochester, N.Y. and lived at 148 Davis St., close to the Public Market. Sammy Gingello would be born 17 years later, on Oct. 24, 1939.

James Gingello (Giglio) Sr. had four children. Anthony Gingello Sr., the oldest of four siblings, was born in 1934; James Gingello Jr. was born in 1936; Salvatore, Sammy G, was born in 1939; and their sister, Michelina, was born in 1941.

Grandpa James Gingello Flees Sicily

In **1922**, my Grandfather James Gingello, at the age of 11 years old, along with his mother, father, brothers and sisters had to flee Sicily, or in Sicilian, "Sicilia," because my grandfather at the young age of 11, killed a man that was trying to steal their food. I don't know who the man was. That's all that was ever spoke, and that only in a whisper, amongst the family.

Grandpa Gingello (Jimmy) never bragged about the situation. No one in the family would ever think about disrespecting Grandpa G. by asking him any questions about it. Grandpa G. did the best he could to provide for his family. He put a roof over their heads, food on the table and clothes on their backs. He was a very hard worker.

Grandpa G. was also an amateur boxer in his younger days. He worked at the Public Market and eventually became a city employee.

October 24, 1939

Salvatore 'Sammy G' Gingello is Born

On **Oct. 24, 1939**, Salvatore "Sammy G" Gingello was born to Angelina (Angie) Gingello and James (Jim) Gingello.

One of the earliest pictures that Gina Gingello had of her dad was a picture taken in **1942** when Sammy was only three years old.

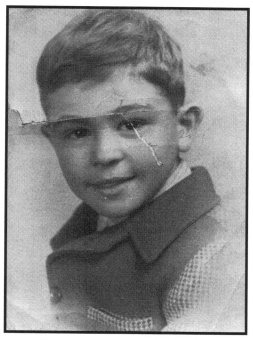

Sammy Gingello in 1942, age 3.

On the left is a 1946 photo taken of James Gingello while he was employed as a Rochester snow plow driver. Sam's father James, like many immigrants of the era, gained employment as a laborer.

**James
Gingello
1946**

James Gingello Fired for Joining Union

On **May 15, 1946,** James Gingello was one of 489 city workers fired because they dared to join a union. Then on **May 23, 1946,** James was one of 208 union members jailed for exercising their right to picket.

The City of Rochester had unjustly laid off (fired) 489 workers in an effort to break unionization efforts. Mass protests developed on Dewey Avenue, across the street from the city's Department of Public Works. The city accused protesters of intimidating city workers and interfering with public health by blocking garbage trucks and preventing garbage collection. (60)

Strike of '46 defended local union progress

By ANTHONY GINGELLO

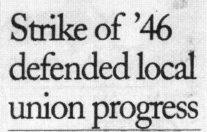

On May 15, 1946, my father, James Gingello, was one of the 489 city workers fired because they dared to join a union. Ten days later, 50,000 Rochester workers walked off their jobs for 22 hours in protest over the firings. Half a century has passed, but the issues that provoked Rochester's general strike of '46 are still with us today.

Gingello

Fifty years later, James's son Anthony was an established union member and labor leader himself. He was the President of the largest city workers union in Rochester, N.Y.

Anthony Gingello wrote an article for the Democrat and Chronicle on the 50th anniversary of the 1946 strike in order to give tribute to his father and all other union members alike.

1946
James Gingello Arrested in Labor Dispute

Labor News on May 31, 1946. Union members were jailed after picketing at the city Department of Public Works. James Gingello, father of Anthony and "Sammy G" Gingello, is second from right.

In **1946** Sammy was only seven years old, his father James Gingello, was employed at the city Department of Public Works. He was a very active union member. On **May 23, 1946**, eight days after getting fired, James was among 208 union members who were jailed on disorderly conduct charges while picketing their employer.

Another union member, Charles Teeter, a city garbage wagon driver, was always accompanied by his brown mongrel dog named "Tippy." So when Teeter was arrested with the other union workers, his dog "Tippy" went with him. Tippy can be seen in the picture above, behind bars, on the bottom left. (27)

Tippy on His Way to Jail.

It seemed that unionism was in the Gingello blood and would remain that way for years to come, with all three of James Gingello's sons becoming involved in organized labor.

Sammy would be affiliated with the Teamsters Union, Anthony would work for the city worker's union for 60 years, leading that union as president for 45 of those years. And James Jr. was also involved with the union right up until his death on March 26, 1969. (28)

More than 5,000 people gathered in Washington Square Park in Downtown Rochester to protest the arrests and show support for the unions.

Rochester snow fighters (snowplow drivers) after returning from Oswego in 1946. James Gingello is standing in the top row on the far left.

14

Holy Redeemer School

In the mid 1940's, the Gingello family was living in the city of Rochester, N.Y. and young Sammy, or "Sonny" (as he was known then), attended the local Catholic school, Holy Redeemer School on Hudson Avenue.

"Sonny" at age 7 in 1946 Holy Redeemer School

"Sonny" in 1947 at age 8.

Sam (circled) at age 7 in the second grade. The picture was taken in 1946 at Holy Redeemer School on Hudson Avenue.

Sam "Sonny" Gingello.

1948 Holy Redeemer Baseball Team

1948 Holy Redeemer Baseball Team. Nine-year old Sammy Gingello is number 5 on the top left.

Sammy's Confirmation in 1950

Following in Catholic tradition, the Gingello family being strict Catholics, Sammy was Confirmed at Holy Redeemer Church on Hudson Avenue in 1950, when he was 11 years old.

Sammy (left) with his sponsor, Frank Torino. Picture was taken at Bobby Rizzo's house on Ryan Avenue in 1950.

1952
Working at the Public Market
13 Years old

My father started working at the Public Market at the age of 13. Mike Laudisa, a police officer at the time, would patrol the neighborhood of the Public Market. He told me how he would give my father a ride in the police car, just for fun. He told me what a great kid my father was and a very hard worker. He has very fond memories of my father, as do most people who were fortunate enough to meet him.

The Public Market is where Sammy first met Red Russotti. Apparently Red began "grooming" Sammy at a very early age. Three years later, in 1955, when Sammy Gingello was only 16 years old, Grandpa Gingello went to Red Russotti and said, "Leave my son alone." He was told, "No."

Well, from working at the Public Market and doing odd jobs, one thing led to another and Red Russotti started taking a liking to him. My father started out as an "earner" and moved his way up the ranks faster than anyone else had previously done, eventually becoming the "Underboss" of the Rochester Mafia.

Gingello Brothers Win Art Awards

In 1953, Division of Playgrounds and Recreation held their annual Poster and Art Contest. Sam and James Gingello both won awards for their art work.

On **Feb. 28, 1953,** the Division of Playgrounds and Recreation, in Rochester, N.Y., held their annual Poster and Art Contest. The contest attracted more than 800 entries from 34 different city playgrounds. There were several different categories that awards were presented for such as best chalk drawing and best pen and ink drawing.

Salvatore Gingello, age 13, won first place for Best Oil Painting. His older brother James, age 16, won second place in the same category. Both brothers were from the Washington Playground. The event was so popular that a fair size newspaper review was printed in the local Democrat and Chronicle newspaper to honor the award recipients. (61)

1954
Sam and Ted Snacki

Sam Gingello, left, and Ted Snacki, Sam's brother-in-law (right), are at Durand Eastman Park in 1954. Sam is 15 years old and Ted is 19.

1955

Left to right is Robert "Robby" Concordia, Joe "Pico" Allesi and Sam "Sonny" Gingello, who is 16 years old here. The picture was taken on Trust Street.

In 1955, Sam "Sonny" Gingello was 16 years old. Two of his best friends were Robert "Robby" Concordia and Joe "Pico" Allesi. The picture on the left shows the boys hanging out on Trust Street.

Later that year Sam's good friend, Robert Concordia, was married. Sam was still only 16 years old at the time he stood up for the wedding.

The picture on the right of Sam Gingello was taken at Robert Concordia's Wedding.

Gina describes this photo as being among her most favorite pictures of her dad.

Sammy Gingello at age 16.

Sammy Gingello at Robert Concordia's Wedding Reception, held at the Sheridan Hotel. They drove to the Reception in Sam's Cadillac. In 1955 Sam was 16 years old.

Wedding photos were taken at Maplewood Park. Sam is in the middle.

1955
Davis Street

Davis Street is where everyone hung out in 1955. The reason being (it had) Joe's Barber Shop, 16th Ward Venetian Club, and Gervasi's Bar and Grill. So if you stayed out all night you could go to Joe's Barber Shop, get a shave, sleep a little, grab something to eat at Gevasi's, and go gambling at the 16th Ward Venetian Club.

✱✱✱✱✱

Tom Meets Dad

Tom Marotta at age 17.

Tom Marotta was 13 years old when he first met my father, who was three years older. Tom got into a fight at Edison Tech High School. On his way home a car pulled up with four guys and all four proceeded to beat up Tom. The following day Tom met my father, and Sam asked him if he had a problem. Tom said, "No problem."

They talked for a while and Sam said to Tom, "Be at the smoking court in the school at 9:45 in the morning. There will be some guys there to meet you to make sure that never happens again." It was a one on one fight, and the friendship began.

Tom had to "go away" for 19 months and 13 days. The next time they saw each other was at the Garden Grill on Norton and Carter Streets. Now Tom was 16 and Sam was 19.

Tom Marotta and Friends

From left to right, are Italian Mike, Angelo Misuraca, Tommy Marotta, Skip Battaglia, Russell, and Sam Cutia.

"That's when Tom Marotta was 13 or 14 years old. That's what he looked like when he first met my father. And yes he's the one with the cigarette hanging out of his nose instead of his mouth."

Sammy in 1956 at 17 years old

Sammy (left) with his friend Tony Serra (right). The picture was taken at the Serra home on Mark Street. Both young men were 17 years old.

Sitting, are Tony Serra; Sam's sister Michelina (Mickey), 14 years old; Angela Gingello, Sam's mother. Sam is standing.

1956

Tony Serra and Sam G. (picture was taken in 1956 on Mark Street)

The Serra / DiPalermo Wedding

Sam G's good friend, Tony Serra, married Sam's cousin, JoAnn DiPalermo. Sam was the Best Man and Sam's sister, Michelina (Mickey), was JoAnn's Maid of Honor.

From left to right is Michelina (Mickey) Gingello, Maid of Honor; JoAnn DiPalermo Serra, the Bride; Tony Serra, the Groom, and Sam Gingello, the Best Man at the Serra Wedding.

1956 - Sammy at age 17, and Jim Jr. age 20

Sammy (right) and his brother Jimmy Jr. (left) were closer than any two brothers have ever been. (Picture was taken on Mark Street.)

Pictured, are Tony Gingello Sr. (left), in his early 20's, and Joseph (Snuffy) Grock (right), at a Pennsylvania Avenue bar owned by a Mr. Cerniglia. Gina's Uncle Tony worked there and Gina's dad (Sam) hung around there.

They called it "The Bar on the Corner," although that was not its real name. The Gingello's also owned a Bar and Grille on the corner of Central Park at Hebard Street.

Gingello's Bar & Grille
166 Central Park

Gingello's Bar & Grille was located at 166 Central Park, at the corner of Hebard Street in Rochester, N.Y. Today there is an empty lot where the bar once stood. The building on the right is 172 Central Park and the closest house on the left (not pictured) is 156 Central Park.

"It has been confirmed to me that the Gingello brothers had their own bar on Central Park called Gingello's Bar & Grille. My Uncle Jimmy (Junior) and my Uncle Tony would run it during the day, and then at night time Tom Marotta and George Triesta would run it. At nighttime it was a strip club. It was the only black strip club in the entire City of Rochester at the time."

The bar closed in 1969 after losing their liquor license due to three Alcoholic Beverages Control law violations, which included a shooting. (84)

Bar Closed – Wrong Kind Of Shots

Gingello's Bar & Grill Inc at 166 Central Park has lost its liquor license because of three Alcoholic Beverages Control law violations which included a shooting on the premises.

Oct. 12, 1969
Democrat and
Chronicle

August 29th 1959
Snacki / Gingello Wedding

On **Aug. 29, 1959,** Sam's younger sister, Michelina, was married to Tadeusz (Ted) Snacki at St. Andrew's Church on Portland Avenue. Sam was the "Best Man." Sam was 20 years old and his sister had just turned 18 on August 18th, less than two weeks prior to the wedding. (68)

August 29, 1959
Snacki / Gingello Wedding

At left is the Michelina Gingello bride photo that appeared in the Democrat and Chronicle newspaper.

Sam Gingello (left), 20 years old, was best man at his sister's wedding.

Mrs. Tadeusz Snacki
. . . *Michelina Gingello*

MISS MICHELINA Gingello, daughter of Mr. and Mrs. James Gingello Sr. of Trust Street, became the wife of Tadeusz Snacki, son of Mr. and Mrs. Alexander Snacki of Seabrook Street, in a ceremony performed Aug. 29 in St. Andrew's Church.

Michelina and
Tadeusz Ted Snacki

1959 Pontiac - Sam's
brother Jim Jr.'s car

August 29, 1959
Snacki / Gingello Wedding Reception

Sam (on the right) makes a toast to his sister at the wedding luncheon, which was held on Empire Boulevard at Anthony's Restaurant on Aug. 29, 1959. He was making a toast because he was the best man.

Saint Andrews Church on Portland Avenue on Aug. 29, 1959. On the left side rear is my dad. (Sam G.)

Sams parents and Gina's grandparents, Angelina Angie Gingello and James Jim Gingello, dance at their daughter's reception at the Polish Home on Hudson Avenue.

Sam, on the right, in the Receiving line at the Reception at the Polish Home.

1959
Al Capone Movie

In 1959 when Sam "Sonny" Gingello was 20 years old he took his girlfriend and future wife Janice to the movies. They saw an Al Capone movie. Sammy told Janice after the movie:

"Some day I am going to be just like him."

1961

Oct. 23, 1961 - Anthony Gingello (above), Ontario Street Garage employee, observes wrecked car that killed a man at the corner of Driving Park and Lake Avenue. Photo taken at John's Paint Shop at 4 Niagara St. (69)

This is the house that my parents built right before they got married. It was their first home. My mother was 25 and my father was 24.The home is located on Wolcott Avenue in Gates. The number of the house was 51. I took my mother by it recently and she said it looked exactly the same, except for the garage door was different.

Sammy Gingello and his new bride Janice had this house built at 51 Wolcott Ave. in Gates in June of 1962, and moved in shortly thereafter.

To the best of her recollection, my mother said the house started being built in June 1962 and she believes it was completed at the end of September of 1962 and they were married in October of 1962.

October 27, 1962
Sammy G's Wedding
at St. Francis Xavier Church

Above is Best Man John Asito, on the right, who adjusts Sam's tie before the wedding ceremony. Below are Sam Gingello's Bride, Janice Gennell on the right and her sister Gloria Lana (left).

Sammy Gingello and Janice Gennell at the alter getting married in St. Francis Xavier Church on Oct. 27, 1962.

Janice and Sam (above). Below, the Bride and Groom pose with both sets of parents. On the left are Janice's parents, Anthony "Musty" Gennell and his wife Vincenzina (Jennie) Gennell, and on the right are Sammy's parents, Angelina (Angie) Gingello and James (Jim) Gingello.

Sam and Janice's Wedding Reception was held at St. Standislaus. Below, Janice Gingello (Bride), Sam Gingello and Sam's Best Man, John Asito, greet guests.

Goofing around at Sam's Wedding reception. On the left is
Tony Gingello, Sammy's brother. In the center is Richard
Marino, and on the right is Sammy Gingello. The Reception
was held at St. Stanislaus. (Shots-Pizza-Peanuts-Beer-Cookies
and Cake.)

The Groomsmen

My father's wedding picture with the groomsmen. From left to right
are   James "Dada" Cignilia, John "Flowers" Fiorino, Lawrence
"Larry" Pellegrino, my Grandpa Gingello, James Gingello, my father
(Sam Gingello), John Asito, Anthony Gingello, Richard Marino, Tedi-
ous Snacki, and James Junior Gingello.

10 Arrested as Youths Scuffle with Police

Ten persons were arrested to grab his gun and night Anthony Calari, 19 of 3!
during a near riot at Norton stick. [Cascade Place; Salvatoi
Street and Goodman Street The youth told O'Connor Gingello, 22, of 50 Page Ave
North about 3 a.m. yesterday. he was the one who had to Irondequoit, and Jame

Early in the morning on **Sept. 8, 1963,** a large group of youths were congregating around a locked, parked car containing a passed out young woman. A complaint was called in and police responded.

When the officer attempted to disperse the gang, one man tried to grab his gun and nightstick. The man, who was identified as John Fiorito (Fiorino), 20, told the officer that he was the one who had to move. Fiorino was promptly arrested and charged with disorderly conduct.

When the officer attempted to place Fiorino in his patrol car he was hit and kicked several times by the other members of the gang of unruly youths. Once in the patrol car the gang rocked the patrol car and pelted it with apples.

Ten men were arrested on disorderly conduct charges but four of them escaped police custody before they could be taken to police headquarters for processing. Among those arrested were Salvatore Gingello, 23, of 50 Page Ave. and Jimmy Cristo, age 20.

6 in Near Riot Sentenced to 'Weekend Jail'

Four youths and two men involved in a near riot outside a restaurant at Goodman and Norton streets Sept. 8 were sentenced yesterday to serve the next four weekends in the Monroe County Penitentiary.

Before the month ended, six of the ten men arrested for scuffling with police were found guilty and sentenced for their roles in the melee.

On **Sept. 30, 1963,** four youths and two men, including Salvatore Gingello and Jimmy Cristo, were each sentenced to serve the next four weekends in the Monroe County Penitentiary. They were to surrender on Friday evenings at 6 p.m. and they were to be released on Sunday evenings at 6 p.m. for the entire month of **October 1963.** (30)

December 3, 1963
Gina Gingello was Born

1964
Sam and Gina

On the left is Sammy and his daughter Gina at Grandma Gingello's house on Mark Street in 1964. Sammy is 25 years old and Gina is about one year old.

Below is Gina and Sam at 50 Page Ave.

Joey DiMarie's Father's Joint (1964)
Sam Deals Cards

Joey DiMarie's father's Joint was on the corner of Lewis Street and Scio Street Sam used to deal cards at the joint in the winter time when he was laid off from his trucking job.

The Fire at the Lewis Street Joint

My father once ran a joint on the corner of Scio Street and Lewis Street. There was a fire there in 1965. Today it is just a vacant lot. Through the years I've heard things about that fire. It was always just bits and pieces of the story but this is what I was able to put together.

There was some arguing over opening and running the gambling joints. For some reason my father had set someone's pool table on fire inside of their joint. They retaliated by setting his joint on fire. The only difference was that what my father did was just destroy a pool table. What happened to my father and John Fiorino was a Molotov cocktail thrown through the window, trapping them inside the burning joint, leaving them trying to find a way out.

According to the story, they broke a window and were able to escape that way. John had suffered some minor burns, but my father got the worst of it and was burnt up considerably more than John. So John drove my father to my mother's house on Page Avenue and was able to get my father in the house and lie him down.

When my mother saw him (my father) she said to John, "Is he dead?" John did his best to reassure her that no, he wasn't dead. Finally my father opened his eyes and told John to take him to Jimmy's (Jr.) house. My mother and John tried to talk him out of it, but my father insisted. So John took him there.

My mother had to stay home because I was sleeping and I was only two years old at the time, and neither my mother or my father wanted me to see him like that. Grandma G. went to Jr.'s home and from there they took my father to the hospital. They told the hospital some story about him smoking near a gas can.

When he was released from the hospital my Uncle Jr. called my mother to let her know that my father would be fine. She asked who was going to bring him home and was told that he was going to Ma's house (Grandma G.) because he did not want Gina to see him yet.

The other thing wrong with starting my father's joint on fire was that the joint was the bottom half of a house. Innocent people were living upstairs. If whoever torched the joint thought that it would be unoccupied at that time of night, they certainly failed to take into consideration the people upstairs. Thank God they all got out of the house safely.

August 1965

This photo is John Asito (left) Marty Allen (center) and Sam Gingello on the right. The date on back of photo says August 1965.

John Asito, left. I'm not sure of the name of the guy in the middle. He was a boxer and my father is on the right.

Mid-Sixties
at The Flamingo Hotel
Las Vegas, Nevada

From left to right, are Jimmy Cristo, John Asito, unknown woman, Sam Gingello, and James Pizzo (Jimmy Pitts), who was a stunt double for actor Robert Taylor and starred in black and white movies; the last gentleman is Anthony Amico, a Pit Boss at the casino. The place was the Flamingo Hotel in Las Vegas, sometime during the mid sixties.

1967 Sam and Janice are Divorced

On **May 8, 1967,** paperwork was filed to initiate a divorce between Salvatore Gingello and Janice Gennell Gingello. In less than one week the divorce was finalized. According to Gina, "My mother made him go to Mexico to get a quick divorce. It was final on May 11, 1967."

1968 Gina and Sam

Gina and her father Sam Gingello at 12 Manitou St. in 1968. Gina is five years old and Sam is 29 years old.

Chapter 2:
'Sammy G' The Gambler

The Young Man's Social Club on Bay Street / My Childhood

"The 'Young Man Social Club,' located at 606 Bay St. was one of my father's joints. Above is the way it looks today. The joint was located in the upper part of the building so you would walk up the stairs to the where he had the joint."

Gina Gingello

It was just like you see in the movies. For all cookout occasions you spent time with dad's friends. It was just normal. There were no outsiders, ever!

As soon as I was able to walk, dad let me loose in the joints. Everyone of course was very nice to me. All the guys would play with me. I really loved going there. It was another thing that was just "normal." I would play shuffleboard and walk around the tables while the guys were playing cards. That's how I learned to play blackjack. All normal!

Clifford Avenue Joint

I remember a man named Uncle Bootsy. What a nice guy. All the guys at that time were stealing eight track tapes from each others' cars. Dad would make me be the lookout for him as he was rifling through whoever's car. Boy would he get mad when he would find his own tapes missing, but that was the game. Boys will be boys.

Cozy Corner on Clifford Avenue

At the bar across the street Dad would have a cocktail and he would order me a "kiddy cocktail." My mother would take me there early in the evening on Christmas Eve to go see him. Everyone would be there to have their Christmas drink together. Then my mother and myself would go to Mama Rosa's house on Bay Street, where her side of the family lived.

We would have the seven fishes and go to the midnight Mass at St. Francis Church and then walk back to Mama Rosa's and have everything. Peppers and onions and sausage, all the fish, all kinds of meat and desserts. You name it, we had it.

We would all sleep over at Mama Rosa's house, and then on Christmas morning we would go back to our own homes. At that time I lived at 12 Manitou St. At home, when we walked in the house, we saw the silver Christmas tree that dad had bought and fell in love with. There were all kinds of gifts under the tree for my mother and myself, and of course dad. He would go there (to the house) before we got home in the morning and be waiting for us to get home. Just our little family.

Even though my mother and father were divorced, they were the best of friends. He would call her his big sister because she was a year older than him.

Gaming Raid Nets 18

Gaming Raid Nets 18

Six detectives of the Special Criminal Investigation Unit yesterday broke up what they termed the "daily matinee" blackjack game at the Northeast Home Improvement Association, 257 Bay St., and arrested 18 men.

On **Feb. 1, 1968,** six detectives of the special Criminal Investigation Unit raided the Northeast Home Improvement Association, located at 257 Bay St. and broke up the "daily matinee" blackjack game that was in progress. They arrested 18 men.

Salvatore Gingello, of 1623 Clifford Ave., was arrested and charged with "promoting and advancing gambling." Bail was set at $750. Seventeen other men were arrested and charged with being "inmates of a gambling place." Their bail was set at $15 per man. Among those arrested as inmates were Angelo Amico, Angelo Fico, Sam Greco, Thomas Alaimo, Joseph Geniola, and others.

Sammy pleaded guilty to violating a city ordinance that same month. (31)

Blow Aimed at Gamblers

6 Clubs on Spot

Blow Aimed At Gamblers

By TOM RYAN

Rochester police have asked the state attorney general's office to revoke the charters of six clubs which they claim are fronts for gambling activities.

The vice investigators say the move could hand local gamblers their biggest blow in years.

To support their case, city police on Friday submitted to the attorney general gambling convictions they have obtained in City Court against operators and/or officers of these clubs during the past year.

The plan to attack the chartered club gambling problem this way was conceived

State Street Social Club, 803 State St., Frank DiPonzio the said operator.

Northway Social Club, 234 Portland Ave., Charles and Murphy Russo the said operators.

In **June of 1968,** Rochester police petitioned the state attorney's office to revoke the charters of six clubs that they claimed were fronts for gambling operations. To support their case, police waited until an ample amount of gambling convictions were obtained at each location before submitting the petition.

One of those clubs was the Sixteenth Ward Veterans Club, which formerly operated from the Goodman Novelty Shop at 1313 Goodman Ave. Salvatore Gingello was the club's president. (32)

Sixteenth Ward Veterans Club, which had operated in the now-defunct Goodman Novelty Shop, 1313 Goodman St. N., Salvatore Gingello the said club president.

Gambling Raid Nets 31 Arrests

Gambling Raid Nets 31 Arrests

Police raided two alleged gambling spots on **Sept. 8, 1968**. One of those places was the North End Mutual Improvement Association, a state chartered "social club", which was located at 606 Bay St. They seized card tables, betting slips, and other gambling paraphernalia.

The club's operators were Joseph "Snuffy" Grock, 54, and Salvatore Gingello, 28, of 1203 Bay St. Both men were arrested, along with Michael Lipani. The three men were all charged with advancing gambling and possession of bookmaking records, in violation of the city's anti-gambling ordinance. (33)

Gingerbread Man (1968)

I learned the story of the Gingerbread Man in kindergarten. My dad was so proud of me he made me tell that story to everyone. I told it to the whole family and all the guys in the joint. This one time some guy pulled his car up along the side of our car and my father told this guy to park his car and come back to ours because he wanted me to tell the guy the Gingerbread Man story.

I guess I used a lot of expression when I told the story because dad would give everyone a heads up to watch my eyes. He would get the biggest smile every time I told the story. I can still see it in my head right now. It was just a dad who was proud of his little girl telling the Gingerbread Man story.

Dance Recitals (Grades 1-3)

My father came to every one of my dance recitals. I do have to say sometimes he was a little late, but he was always there by the time I was on stage. I always looked for him, and when I spotted him I would stop dancing and wave to him. Even at a young age nothing mattered to me but my dad.

After the recital was over he would bring me flowers and tell me how great I did. He would give me hugs and kisses and then leave. I never thought he was telling the truth because I wasn't that good, but I guess in his eyes I was.

My Birthdays

My birthdays were always very special to my dad.

He always had his own special message put on my birthday cake, "TO MY LITTLE PRINCESS," "TO MY LITTLE LOVE," "DADDY'S LITTLE GIRL." My cakes were always so beautiful and either had frilly dressed dolls or ballerinas on them. And of course a shopping spree always went along with it.

Parenting

When I messed up (growing up) my dad would always allow me to plead my case, which I usually did VERY VOCALLY. He would then ask, "Are you finished?" Of course I wasn't, I always had something else to say. And then he would ask again, "Are you finished?"

But once I said I was finished he would say "Okay my turn," and look at me. He would never raise his voice at all. The only thing he had to do was raise one eye brow and I knew to shut the Hell up. Very calmly he would explain to me how things were going to go. I would never think of questioning him or ask him why whenever he had that one eye brow raised.

It wasn't that I feared my dad, I respected him and I feel he respected me enough to always hear me out. But of course, at the end of the day, what dad said, went. He was not only my dad he was my best friend. I could talk to him about everything and anything at all. Probably some of the girl stuff made him a little uncomfortable; but I have to say, when I "became a woman" at the age of 11 he brought me flowers and said, "No matter what, you will always be daddy's little girl." And he was a trooper dealing with all of my mood swings.

Moral Values

Beginning at a very young age, moral values and respect were instilled in me. Even though I was spoiled, every winter, spring, summer and fall I had a new wardrobe. Things weren't just given to me, I had to earn them with good grades and good behavior.

My dad was "in the business" as we all know. But first and foremost he was a father that taught me values. That is one of the reasons why after he died it wasn't as hard as you would think to make the transition from enjoying the finer things in life, to going without.

I started babysitting at 12 years old and continued to work into my early 50's until I tore a rotator cuff so bad that I lost 75% mobility in my arm.

Altar Girls

I remember when Patty Sofia and myself talked Father Golden, the parish priest at St. Francis Xavier, into making us "Alter Girls." It wasn't fair that there wasn't any Altar Girls. *We were told there was a reason they are called Altar Boys.* Well, if you know Patty and myself, we didn't like to take "no" for an answer. So we became the very first "Altar Girls" in the city of Rochester.

My father was so proud. Mass had just started when here comes walking in my father and Joe "The Hop" Rossi, wearing suits and ties with long black trench coats. Their hats, of course, were in their hands and they sat in the second pew from the front.

'Man Called in Social Club Probe'

SALVATORE GINGELLO

Man Called
In Social
Club Probe

Sam was served a subpoena on **June 11, 1969** directing him to appear at the attorney general's office to answer questions in regard to a police investigation into gambling. Specifically in question was Gingello's relationship with the 16th Ward Veterans Club, which police claimed was a front for a gambling operation. (34)

Sam Gingello's Home Raided

On **July 9, 1969**, Sammy Gingello's home on Plank Road was raided, and Sam was arrested for possession of gambling records and promoting gambling. The raid was the culmination of a month long investigation into gambling operations believed to be controlled by organized crime. (35)

At Penfield Home
Gambling Raid Nets 3 Suspects

By TOM RYAN

A small task force of police and FBI agents raided the Penfield home of a local gambling figure yesterday morning, arresting three men and seizing more than $3,100 in cash and a large quantity of betting slips.

As the raiding force entered, two of the suspects were tallying bets on an adding machine in the kitchen of the Salvatore Gingello residence at 1146 Plank Road, investigators reported.

Horse bet slips, baseball parlay bets and a bank bag containing $747 were on a kitchen table with the adding machine, according to Dets....

Penfield house raided by police yesterday.

1969

Sammy and Gina Gingello on Manitou Street in 1969. Sammy is 30 years old and Gina is six years old.

Manitou Street is darkened in the center of the map and runs between Fernwood Avenue and Clifford Avenue, opposite Aurora Street.

Raid at Bay Street Club Nets Gambling Arrests

Raid at Bay Street Club Nets Gambling Arrests

The following month, on **Aug. 14, 1969,** just one month after raiding Sam Gingello's home, investigators raided the Bay Street Social Club, located at 606 Bay St., netting a virtual who's who in the Rochester gambling community. But Sammy G. was conspicuously absent and escaped arrest. Sources said that he was in Las Vegas on a gambling junket.

Among those arrested were John Fiorino, Angelo Amico, Sam Pizzo, Charles Fiannaca, George Trieste, Charles Russolesi, and Joseph Rossi. The club was previously raided the year before, on Sept. 7, 1968, when a dozen men were arrested. [36]

October 23, 1969
Sammy G and Four Others
Convicted of Disorderly Conduct

Sammy G., Four Others Convicted

By TOM RYAN

Five men arrested last March after a confrontation with Police vice investigators in a parking lot at the Bay Street Social Club, 606 Bay St., yesterday were found guilty of disorderly conduct.

City Court Judge Wilmer J. Patlow set sentencing for Nov. 7.

The five — Salvatore (Sammy G.) Gingello, 29, of 1146 Plank Road, Penfield; his brother, Anthony, 34, of 21 Lemanz Drive, Gates; Joseph (Snuffy) Grock, 54, of 690 Wi-

nona Blvd., Irondequoit; John Polino, 67, of 3413 Dewey Ave., Greece, and Salvatore Rivoli, 46, of 161 Newcomb St. were commited free in $500 bail each.

The Penal Law violation of which they were found guilty carries a maximum sentence of a $250 fine or 15 days in the penitentiary.

They originally were charged with obstructing governmental administration, a class "A" misdemeanor which allows for a maximum sent-

Please turn page

On **Oct. 23, 1969,** Sammy Gingello and four other men were found guilty of disorderly conduct because they allegedly interfered with a police investigation in the parking lot of the Bay Street Social Club, located at 606 Bay St. They were all originally charged with "obstructing government administration."

The judge found the men guilty under a special section of the law that covers persons who "create a hazardous or physically dangerous condition by any act which serves no purpose." Apparently strategically placing cars in your own parking lot to block police cars from entering creates "a hazardous or physically dangerous condition which serves no purpose." (37)

The Mahoney / Lupo Connection

William Mahoney and Billy Lupo were friends. And according to the local newspaper they were rumored to be business partners as well. But, Mahoney owed Lupo money. He had borrowed $5,000 at the standard "vig" of 6 for 5, which meant he owed $6,000.

So, Chief of Detectives William Mahoney used to take Billy Lupo, who was a Captain in the Rochester Mafia, around town to rob homes in his police car. Mahoney would listen to the police scanner so he would know if a robbery was being reported, in which case he would beep the horn to alert Lupo.

Together they would also shake down hookers at the Keyboard Lounge. But there was a confrontation at the Keyboard lounge one day between Bill Mahoney and Billy Lupo. At some point William (Back Room Bill) Mahoney, who was known for slapping around suspects and beating confessions out of them, was slapped around himself by Billy Lupo. Getting confessions was not the only thing slapping people around was good for, it was also quite useful for expediating payments of debt.

Shortly after this incident, Billy Lupo was murdered. Lupo was very paranoid about who he rode around with, which would imply that he was killed by someone that he trusted. (70)

2 More Grills Face Charges by SLA on Morals

The State Liquor Authority yesterday charged two more Rochester restaurants with permitting women to solicit bar patrons.

In April 1962, the State Liquor Authority charged the owners of the Keyboard Lounge with allowing prostitutes to solicit bar patrons.

December 7, 1969
$100,000 Stolen from Sammy G's House

Says 100G to Pay Bet Debt Was Stolen From Home

Rochester, N.Y., Dec. 7 (AP)— A suitcase allegedly containing more than $100,000 to pay off gambling debts was reported today by its caretaker as having been stolen from his home.

Police said Salvatore Gingello, 29, of suburban Penfield, who is awaiting trial on charges of possession of gambling records and of promoting gambling, told them that the money was to have been flown to Las Vegas to pay off gambling debts incurred by 130 Rochester residents on a recent trip there.

Gingello said the money was in $50 and $100 bills. He told police that the money was given to him by members of the Mato Flyers Club to satisfy loans taken out to pay the Las Vegas bills.

Gingello, who is an officer of the club, told police that the only people who knew where the money was located in his house were officers of the club and associates in Las Vegas.

Dec. 9, 1969 Daily News
New York, New York

On **Dec. 7, 1969,** Salvatore Gingello reported the theft of a suitcase full of money from his home on Plank Road. The suitcase containing $100,000 in $50 and $100 bills was supposed to be flown to Las Vegas to pay off gambling debts incurred by 130 Rochester residents. (38)

According to Gina, this incident occurred while Sam was away from his home attending her birthday party, which was on a Sunday. Gina had turned six on Wednesday, Dec. 3, 1969. Her birthday party was held the following Sunday, Dec. 7, 1969, the same day as the theft.

Billy Lupo Found Slain

The body of William J. Lupo was found on **Feb. 18, 1970**, a bullet fired in the back of his head from behind. Lupo had been described as a Cosa Nostra figure by the State Investigation Com-

Rochester Man, Linked to Mafia, Slain in His Auto

Rochester, Feb. 18 (AP)—A bullet fired into his head from behind killed William J. Lupo, 42, described by the State Investigation Commission as a Cosa Nostra figure. Lupo's body was found today

mission. Lupo was the next door neighbor of Salvatore "Sammy G." Gingello. (39)

1970

Gambling Club Shut By Judge

Gambling Club Shut By Judge

City Court Judge Culver K. Barr yesterday evicted the Bay Street Social Club from its headquarters.

The club, which police say is a center for local organized gambling activities, is at 606 Bay St.

The decision, which probably will be appealed, means that the club will have to vacate the premises by Monday or marshals will deposit its equipment on the street.

Judge Barr's decision was made at the request of the Valguarnera Society, which owns the building and rents the second floor to the club.

The club is managed by Salvatore "Sammy G" Gingello, 30, of 1146 Plank Road, Penfield. Police describe Gingello as a close associate of Cosa Nostra figures here.

Gingello's home is next to that of William J. "Billy" Lupo, who was discovered dead of three bullet wounds in his head on a street of Norton Street in the city two weeks ago.

SALVATORE GINGELLO
... gets evicted

A gambling parlor managed by Salvatore Gingello, better known as The Bay Street Social Club, was shut down by City Court Judge Culver Bar on **March 5, 1970**. Police claimed the club was a center for local organized gambling activities. (40)

Gambling Trial

On **July 24, 1970,** Sammy Gingello's gambling trial for his July 9, 1969 arrest began its fourth day. A detective was questioned about allegedly nearly knocking over Mrs. Salvatore Gingello during the raid that occurred at her Plank Road home.

Sammy Gingello, along with Joseph Rossi, 31, and James Greco, 28, were being tried on charges of promoting gambling and possession of gambling records. (41)

Sammy G's Gambling Probation a First

In **early August,** Sammy was found guilty of both gambling charges. He was sentenced on **Aug. 26, 1970**. For the first count of "promoting gambling," Sam was given a $1,000 fine and placed on probation for three years. For the second count, "possession of gambling records," Sam was given a 90 day prison sentence. If he violated probation he would be subject to an additional year in prison. (42)

1970

Sammy G. Arrested for Speeding

While out on bail awaiting an appeal on a gambling conviction, Salvatore Gingello was picked up and arrested again, this time for speeding. He was accused of leading plainclothes detectives that were surveilling him on a high speed chase.

According to detective John Grande he chased Gingello on the Eastern Expressway at speeds up to 95 miles per hour. Gingello was finally stopped on the Troup-Howard Street Bridge.

At this time, according to the newspaper and police, Salvatore Gingello was known only as an "associate" of organized crime figures in Rochester. [43]

1970-1971 (7-8 years old)
12 Manitou Street
Dad Meets Frank Sinatra

I remember my mother waking me up out of bed to get on the phone with my father. It was like 3 o'clock in the morning and I was still half asleep. I could hear the excitement in his voice. "Are you there," he was saying. "Yes daddy I'm here, what is going on," I said.

He says, "I am in New York City in a little bar and you will never guess who just walked in and I had a drink with." "I don't know, who," I responded. "Frank Sinatra," he said. I was so happy for him because he was so excited.

He told me he was just sitting having a drink and in comes Frank Sinatra with another guy. They had a drink together, exchanged a few pleasant words, and went about their business. And the first thing dad did was call me. We said our good nights and our I Love You's and he told me he would see me in a couple of days when he got back home.

I had the little kids table and chairs set up in the living room. Dad would sit with me on his little chair and me on mine and we would have dinner together.

Italian-American Civil Rights League
Pickets Federal Building

D&C Photo by Dick Haun

Italian-American Civil Rights League picketed Federal Building 2 hours to protest Brooklyn arrest.

Italian Rights Group Pickets FBI

The Italian-American Civil Rights League picketing at the Federal Building on April 23, 1971 in Downtown Rochester.

In the early seventies, The Italian-American Civil Rights League was gaining strength throughout major U.S. cities, and Rochester, N.Y. was one of them. My father had a part in organizing a protest held in Downtown Rochester. (88)

The New York based Italian American Civil Rights League gained its strength as a national organization by involving itself in grass roots community projects in each of the major cities, attracting new members.

Sam Gingello (left) and Frank Valenti at The Italian-American Civil Rights League demonstration in Downtown Rochester in 1971.

Above is an
original sticker
for Chapter 21
Rochester, N.Y.
of the Italian
American Civil
Rights League.

Sam Gingello and Frank Valenti oversee the demonstration of the Rochester Chapter of The Italian-American Civil Rights League that they organized in Downtown Rochester in 1971.

Gina remembers attending this protest with her father and she also remembers that he let her have her own sign to protest with.

The first permanent officers of the Italian-American Civil Rights League, elected last night, are: president, Joseph Costanza; vice president, Vincent Rollo, and secretary-treasurer, Richard Marino.

The following month, May of 1971, the Rochester Chapter of the Italian-American Civil Rights League elected its own officers, as pictured on the left. Elected were President, Joseph Costanza; Vice-President Vincent Rollo and Secretary-Treasurer Richard Marino. (89)

1971 Gina's First Holy Communion

Janice and Sammy Gingello with their daughter Gina in 1971, at Gina's First Holy Communion. The picture was taken at Amalfi's Party House on St. Paul Boulevard. Sam was 32 years old, Janice was 33 years old, and Gina was eight years old.

In **1971**, when Gina was eight years old, she made her First Holy Communion. Gina remembers her dad as always being there for her and participating in all her milestones.

"The day of my Communion Party there were over 100 people there. We sat at the head table. I was in the middle of my mother and father. Grandma and Grandpa G. sat next to my father and Grandma and Grampa Gennell sat next to my mother. My father stood up and made a toast. 'I'd like to thank everyone for coming and joining in the celebration of Gina's Holy Communion.'

He then made me stand up on my chair and ask everyone to raise their glasses and he whispered in my ear and told me to say 'CHINDON,' which means may you live 100 years!"

1971

Sam Gingello and daughter Gina, who was
seven or eight years old in this photo.

Sammy G in the Pen

On **Aug. 26, 1971,** Sammy G was found guilty of harassing a police officer and he was sentenced to serve 15 days in jail. But Sammy was released, pending an appeal, after serving a mere six hours of that sentence.

Sam Gingello was originally accused of disorderly conduct. He allegedly used profanity to a police officer during a routine traffic stop where he was a passenger in an automobile. Gingello was found not guilty of disorderly conduct, but guilty of harassment instead. The appeal was expected to address whether or not a person accused of disorderly conduct can be found guilty of harassment. (44)

Growing Up on Manitou Street

I couldn't have asked for a better childhood. I lived at 12 Manitou St. until the fourth grade. Me and my mom lived in her parents' house in the upstairs apartment. My grandparents owned two homes on Manitou Street, so they lived across the street. In the downstairs apartment in our house lived Betty and Lou Colangelo. They were somehow related to Joey Tiraborelli.

It was like one big family on Manitou Street. Stephany Gangarosa married John Quirino. The Casserino's were already like family. We knew them from Page Avenue where my mother, my father and myself used to live when I was a baby. David Casserino and Roxanne (Rocky) had their first child on Manitou Street. I became Godmother to their second son, Jonathon (John). My childhood best friend was Bessie Quirino. Nick Fosco lived on the corner of Manitou and Fernwood. We weren't just neighbors on that street, we were all family.

There was the Casserino family, the Gangarosa family, the Quirino family, and little Karen Robinson. And I can't leave out the Harris family. They were the first African-American family to move onto our street. Everyone treated them like they had lived there always, especially my father. They were a family of six with four children. Mr. Eddie B. Harris was a machinist.

Nobody locked their doors. We would walk in and out of each other's homes. I do remember sometimes after my father came home from prison, that when we were outside playing that some parents would tell their kids not to go near my dad's car. At the time I just figured it was because me and my dad were talking, but later I found out that wasn't the reason at all. My father did not like me playing football or baseball in the street, especially with the boys. You see, I was an still am a Tomboy.

My dad would pull down Manitou Street and see the dirt on my face, hands, and cloths. He would just raise that eyebrow and

I knew that it was time to get in the house and take a bath and put a dress on, which of course I would and then he would leave.

Well this one day I was outside playing and he drove by, so I pretended like I was going in the house and he drove away like always. The coast was clear, or so I thought. I went right back playing in the street. Guess who came whipping around the corner. You got it. It was dad, and he was not very happy. I never tried that again.

The Harris Family (18 Manitou Street)

As I previously mentioned, the Harris family was the first African-American family to move onto Manitou Street. Mr. Harris was a machine operator at Benz, and later General Motors. Mrs. Lee A. Harris worked as an Assistant Physical Therapist at Beechwood Nursing Home on Culver Road.

Patrick and Cynthia Harris, two of the four Harris children, both had fond memories of my father when I spoke to them. They remembered when they first moved on the street that my father welcomed them to the neighborhood and always treated them like his own.

Patrick refers to my dad as "Mr. Sammy." He remembered how my dad would pull up and ask them how they were doing and then give them money for ice cream. Also, according to both Patrick and Cynthia, my father talked to Mr. Harris about making some extra money and offered to employ him as a numbers runner.

Mr. Harris politely declined the offer and told my father all he wanted to do was raise his family, and Mr. Sammy told him that he respected that, according to Patrick Harris. Dad also let Mr. Harris know that he and his family were now part of our family. He told Mr. Harris if you ever have any problems with anyone, come see me.

1971
Memory With My Cousin Michelle
and My Father

My cousin Michele was my Uncle Jimmy's (Jr.) youngest child. After he passed away, when she was a baby, her mother took her and moved her to California where my aunt's family lived. My father kept and provided for my uncle's two older children. He sent his sister-in-law anything she needed for Michelle, and he also told her to keep all of the childrens' Social Security checks.

In 1971 Michelle was about three years old when they came back to Rochester to visit. I remember sitting at the kitchen table when my dad walked into the dining room holding this beautiful dark curly haired baby in his arms. He held her so tight that at times she would look at him as if she was saying, "I know you love me," and put her little head back on his shoulder as he was giving her little kisses on her little head and cheek.

Even though my cousin hadn't seen my father since she was an infant, she wasn't scared of him at all. It was like she always knew him. She snuggled in his arms and eventually fell asleep. I was so glad that I was there to see that, to witness such a beautiful moment shared between an uncle and his niece. Both of them in each other's arms, it was just so precious. It was at that moment I realized that dad needed hugs from this beautiful baby as much as she needed hugs from him.

Sammy G Saved From Jail

'Sammy G' Saved From Jail

On **Nov. 15, 1971,** Monroe County Judge John J. Conway signed an order directing the sheriff's department to pick up Salvatore Gingello so that he could begin serving a 90 day sentence that was imposed upon him for a gambling conviction. But a last minute court order signed by an appellate judge in Buffalo gave Gingello a temporary stay in his sentence pending the outcome of his appeal. (45)

SALVATORE GINGELLO
. . . *temporary stay*

On **July 7, 1972,** Sammy lost his appeal. His attorneys claimed that they were denied the right to examine confidential FBI notes that led to Gingello's arrest. The prosecution claimed that disclosure of the notes would jeopardize other cases.

The District Attorney's office said that when the court of Appeals order was received by them they would order Gingello to surrender to begin his term. (46)

Jail Nearer For 'Sammy G'

Sam-Jon Trucking Co.
10 Woodward Street
(Before Jail)

Dad's trucking company was located at 10 Woodward St. I loved going there. When you walked into the garage there were 36 white cap red back dump trucks. He also had his own gas truck. When you walked into the office part of the building there were three desks; Snuffy, Rosie, and my mother each had one.

Above is a picture of 10 Woodward St., my father's garage. The window on the far left was his office window and the window in between the garage door and his office window was where my mother, Rosie, and Snuffy's desks were.

The two way radio sat on the front desk by the door. If dad wasn't there when I got there I would call him on the two-way radio. "Base to car one," I would say. He would always finish doing whatever and come right back to the office. By that time I would be playing in his private office.

On the way in to his office he had a big blackened two-way mirror so you could not see in, but he could see out. Behind the mirror was a huge white leather desk with white buttons and a beautiful red chair. It kinda looked like Santa Clause's chair. There was also a white leather loveseat in there, too.

Of course I would be sitting in his chair and be playing at his desk or swirling around in his chair. I can picture him walking in and looking so handsome. I would jump in his arms, give him a big hug and a big kiss, and then try to get back into the chair before he could. Most of the time we shared, he sat on the chair and I sat on his lap.

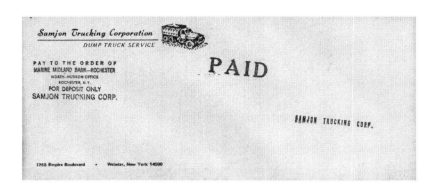

Samjon Trucking Corporation
DUMP TRUCK SERVICE

PAY TO THE ORDER OF
MARINE MIDLAND BANK—ROCHESTER
NORTH-HUDSON OFFICE
ROCHESTER, N.Y.
FOR DEPOSIT ONLY
SAMJON TRUCKING CORP.

PAID

SAMJON TRUCKING CORP.

1750 Empire Boulevard • Webster, New York 14580

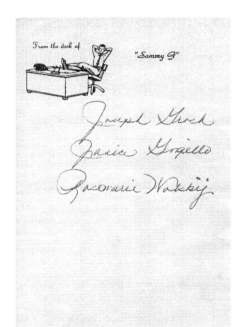

From the desk of   "Sammy G"

The address on the envelope above says 1750 Empire Blvd. Webster, N.Y. 14580.

The stationary on the left says "Sammy G" and has a picture of Sam sitting behind his desk. The names listed on the stationary are Joseph Grock, a gambler who worked for Sam; Janice Gingello, Sam's wife; and Rosemarie, Sam's secretary. All three were employees at Sam-Jon Trucking Co.

Creek Hill Apartments

At the age of 10 we moved to Creek Hill Apartments so we could be closer to dad's office, which was the A-frame house in the back parking lot of the Denonville. So every day after school I would get off the bus and walk to the house (office).

When you walked into the office there were three desks, just like his Woodward Street office. The next room that you entered was a very large room and dad's desk was on the right hand side wall. There were two chairs directly in front of his desk for visitors.

On the other side of the room was a couch, chairs, and a set up like a living room. There was a full kitchen with a table and chairs, etc. It was very nice. I was just a normal kid coming home after school to my mother and father and to be with them where they worked.

Growing Up On Plank Road 1972

What a beautiful house. My father had such good taste; not only in the way he dressed, but also in the furniture and the way he decorated his home. He had a French Provincial Dining Room, a living room, and another room that Italians call 'The Parlor." it was a room that you really never use. It was just there to look at.

In the living room was a large gray sectional couch. In one corner was huge, fully stocked bar. It was gorgeous. Of course there was a counsel TV and in the other corner there was a beautiful fountain. He loved that fountain.

In the back yard was a built in swimming pool with a pink slide. That's right, a pink slide. The outside of the pool was lined with lounge chairs and every few feet along the wooden stockade fence there were artificial palm trees, with lights under them for night time. It was a perfect house for socializing and having cook-outs and parties. And boy did he ever do all of that.

Pig roasts, steak cookouts, and music playing on his juke box in the enclosed sunroom. He would have the croquet game set up. Everyone would be laughing, playing, and drinking. The guys would break each other's balls. Everyone and their families would be there, it was great.

Tom Marotta left and Tony Gingello right tend bar at one of Sam's house parties on Plank Road.

When the sun started to go down we would little by little start moving into the house. A lot of the wives would start leaving with their young children. But the husbands always stayed for a few more drinks.

The one thing I loved the most about going to Plank Road was having a sleepover with my dad. Just him and me. If we did-n't fall asleep on the couch we would sleep in dad's big bed. The bedspread was so heavy that when he tucked me in I could hardly move.

First thing in the morning in the summertime I would want to go see if there were any frogs in the basket in the pool. Nine out of ten times there were. And as I was setting the frogs free, dad was skimming the pool.

Sam and Tony Gingello in the living room at Sam's Plank Road home.

There was one night that always sticks out in my mind. It was after one of my dad's parties. He was tired and had more than a few cocktails in him. He started pretend boxing with me, it was the only boyish thing that my father ever did with me. I think he was playing with me like that in order to teach me how to throw a punch without hurting my wrist.

Then he turned up the stereo as Dean Martin was playing. He started to dance with me and suddenly said, "I have to tell you something. You have an older sister. Her name is Donna." I didn't say anything, but in my heart I knew he was telling me the truth.

After the dance he walked outside to the pool and laid on the lounge chair and was looking around. The lights were glistening off the pool. Because it was dark, the palm tree lights were glowing. He waved his hand across the front of him and said, "The money is all here." I have no idea what he meant by that. He smirked and started to close his eyes. So after a little coaxing I talked him into going inside and we both went to bed.

The next morning, as I was setting frogs free and he was skimming the pool, I asked him who Donna was. He said, "I don't know, Who is Donna?" I didn't question him or push the issue. The look in his eyes was telling me that he had told me the truth the night before. Sometimes Italians don't need to say a word. You learn from the culture to read someone's eyes.

That was another valuable lesson that my father himself taught me. When you are talking to someone and they have trouble maintaining eye contact with you, then the story they are telling you is probably a bunch of lies and you should probably take it with a grain of salt.

Donna Gingello
'How I Found Out Sammy G. was My Father'

My name is Donna Gingello and this is my story, "How I found out Salvatore (Sammy G) Gingello was my father." My mother's name is Beverly Giorgine. She married Peter Giorgine, a Rochester City Police Officer. According to my aunt, my mother Beverly's sister, Peter Giorgine was fully aware that my mother was pregnant with me before they got married. He also knew who my father really was.

As far back as I could remember my mother would take me to my Aunt Rosie's house to visit this man, Sam Gingello, who, I would find out later, was my real father, not Peter Giorgine. My Aunt Rosie was my real father's sister-in-law, my Uncle Tony's wife. So Aunt Rosie, my father (Sam), and myself would sit at her kitchen table and talk. The first question he would always ask me was, "How is your father treating you?"

Before I had the chance to answer I could feel my mother's eyes burning a hole in me and I would get her death stare. So at first I would say "Fine, but I hate him."

He would ask, "Why?"

And I replied, "Because he is a 'pig', a cop."

My father (Sam) would always laugh and say, "Good Girl," with a half smile on his face. Peter Giorgione was very mean to me, even as a small child. How ironic that my stepfather was a cop and my real father is Sam Gingello. My father (Sam) was never aware of the abuse I endured.

I remember I was dating this guy, Mike. My mother hated him. I would always sneak to his house. My mom one day said, "Bring Mike today when we go see Sam."

I said with a dumb look on my face, "Why would you want him to come, you hate him? "

76

She said, "Just bring him." (My mom would always go to his house and try to get me to come home, but at that point I was getting rebellious.) So, I ended up bringing him. When I walked in, there was my father at the table. He really didn't say anything to Mike.

When I went to see Mike I always took a bus to his house. The next day when I went to see him I walked in and was looking around for him. When I found him he was curled in a ball. He told me I had to leave. I asked, "Why?"

He told me, "Mob guys came here and said don't ever see that girl Donna again."

I was puzzled. As I was growing up a lot of things puzzled me. My Aunt, Rosie Gingello, would always take me to buy school clothes every year, shoes, sneaks, etc. She would also take me to see my Grandma G. That's what everyone called her. She was my dad's (Sam) mother. Grandma G. also visited my job at Howard Johnson's every week. I remember she gave me a beautiful bracelet with red rubies.

For years a lot of things bothered me. All through growing up, my step-father, Peter, would always leave my mom and say, "I will take my kids, you take your kid," meaning me. I had a very abusive childhood.

My mother and stepfather, Peter, had an up and down house on Adeane Drive, and Peter's parents lived upstairs. Ever since I was born I had to live upstairs with Peter's parents. As I got older I wanted to go downstairs with my brother and two sisters. That is when this woman, Peter's mother, would beat me with this wooden paddle that she hung on the wall.

I remember my best friend, Vickie Fox, whom I had known since we were four years old, would listen outside the door and hear me getting beat with the paddle. I could not understand why I could not live downstairs with my mom and my siblings.

I asked my mother, when I started getting older, "Why would you give me to her." (Meaning Peter's mother.) My mother said, "Because Peter's mother couldn't have any more children."

Sorry, but that is not what I wanted to hear. My kids are my life. At 13 years old I found out from my cousin, Tony Gingello, the secret he said he could not tell me until I was 18 years old. He told me that the man that I would always visit was my (real) father. At first, I didn't believe him, but Aunt Rosie and Grandma Gingello confirmed it.

My Aunt Rosie put me on her second phone in the bedroom where I listened to her tell my mother that I found out. My mother confirmed what they told me. Sammy Gingello was my father. At that point I was reaching 14 and believe me, I was Hell on wheels.

My father (Sam), even when I did not know he was my dad, was more of a father figure to me than Peter (my stepfather) ever was. Peter had made my childhood a living Hell, along with his parents.

My father (Sam) would also show up at my mother's bar, The Ugly Mug, in Chili. He had his machines there, the games. He would always sit up at the bar talking to me while his body-guard would stand and watch.

At 15 years old I was working at Howard Johnson's, trying to save enough money to move with my boyfriend who had left for the Army. I started sleeping in his car after Peter threw me out of the house. After Sammy, my father, died, my life was a living hell. My mother at one point told me not to come home because he (Peter) was waiting on the stairs for me with a bat. I guess I really intimidated him.

I took the money I had from my Grandmother, who put it in a bank account when I was young, and bought a Pontiac LeMans Sports Coup Car. It was hot! But I always wanted a black Lincoln Continental with the black leather and the tire in the back. Well at 15 years old my mother obviously put the insurance in Peter's

Name, plus I didn't even have a license yet.

So to make a long story short I started taking the car every night. He (Peter) started measuring the seats to see how far back they were to see if I had my uncle, my mom's brother, and his friends in my car. Finally, one day he said I couldn't drive it anymore and that he was selling it, my car, the car that I paid for.

So I got a bat and started smashing the windows out. He called the cops and when the cops came I told them that he (Peter) was beating me. But back then my stepfather was a cop, so the other cops did not care. I left and went to stay at my cousin Virginia's house, which was located behind my house.

The next week when I went back home I walked in and Peter said, "Come here, let me show you what I bought Michele" (my sister). It was a black Lincoln Continental. I asked Peter where the money was from the car he sold and he told me he needed it to buy Michele's car. So the car I bought with my own money he sold and kept the money.

Shortly after that we said our goodbyes. I got on a bus with all my stuff and was on my way to Monterey California, where I would live in a lovely town called Pacific Grove. That's my story in the short version. Put it this way, my childhood was horrendous. My mother was a good mother, but she worked two jobs. So for me my kids come first.

I never had a real family. My other siblings and my mother stick together. But I do have my Gingello family now and we are very close. My sister Gina and cousin Tony have their ups and downs like any other family, but my sister Gina is my life. She sticks by me no matter what. I would do anything for her and she would do anything for me. She has been in and out of my life. She was at my second wedding, but then we drifted apart. Now I am never letting her go. Sometimes she (Gina) acts like me, which I really don't like, but she has balls now and I love her. She is the best. Love you my baby sister, I'm glad you are mine.

In Memory of
My Son Nicholas
(Nicky, Nico, Nucci)

I lost my son on Dec. 31, 2020 at the age of 38 years old in a car accident. My son was the same age as my father Sam, who also lost his life at the age of 38 years old, in a car.

Take care of my baby dad until we meet again.

Donna Gingello

Plank Road and The Spiral Staircase

Sam at home on Plank Road in the early 1970's

At dad's house on Plank Road there was a spiral staircase leading to the crawl space attic. Dad bought me a red velvet maxi coat, and the day he bought it he made me walk up and down those stairs while I was wearing that coat. His smile would get bigger and bigger each time. The look in his eyes when he looked at me were always filled with so much love.

Sam in Las Vegas, early 1970's

Sitting at the table, left to right, are Joseph (Snuffy) Grock, his wife Josie, Susie Geniola, Mary Ann, Sam Gingello, and Joseph Geniola. Bottom left is "Sonny" Celestino, who was not allowed to sit at the main table.

Dad Had A Big Surprise For Me
Lunch with Olivia Newton John

One day dad took me to the Blue Gardenia Restaurant for lunch, which was a normal thing to do. But on this particular day the restaurant was closed to the general public. When we walked in, there was Olivia Newton John sitting at a table on the floor with Nick Fosco.

They were not even in the corner booth that we normally sat in. My dad had his own booth there. Under his booth was a little door with a red phone inside that he would always put on the table when we got there.

Sammy in his car. The picture was taken on Manitou Street by Gina after having lunch with Olivia Newton John in 1975. (Date on back of photo.)

Anyways, there she was, Olivia Newton John. Wow! I just couldn't believe that I was sitting there having lunch with Olivia Newton John. She was very sweet and even brought me a little gift and a card. Unfortunately over the years I lost it.

I loved listening to her talk with her Austin accent. The rumor was that her and Nick Fosco were dating. She would come into town just to see him.

Nick Fosco owned a pizza joint called Nick and Sam's on the corner of Fernwood and Goodman Streets. My friends and I would go there quite often to hang out and grab a slice (of pizza).

WAITRESSES: experience preferred, Nick and Sam's, 1313 N. Goodman.

Nick and Sam's Pizza joint was located at 1313 Goodman St. North. It was the exact same location of Broadway Cavagrotti's former Novelty Shop / gambling parlor. Broadway was murdered in 1967.

So one day Patty Sofia, Cheryl Tiberio and myself walked in and who was sitting in the last booth, Olivia. She called me over. She was as happy to see me as I was to see her. This was after my dad had passed away. I asked her if I could bring my friends over and introduce them to her. She said, "Sure." So I did and they were both thrilled. I never saw Olivia again after that, but I heard her and Nick Fosco always remained friends. (71)

Olivia Newton John

The Cozy Corner Bar

Some of the boys at the Cozy corner bar on Clifford Avenue. The exact date the picture was taken is unknown, but it is believed to been taken sometime between 1974 and 1976. Standing at the top left is Uncle Bootsy "Boobsie" and Tommy Rino. Bottom row, left to right, are Orlando "Orly" Paone, an unidentified man, Joseph "Joey" Trieste, and John Fiorino.

The Cozy Corner Bar was owned by Orlando "Orly" Paone, Donny Paone's father, until about 1976. It was located on Clifford Avenue, directly across the street (kiddy-corner) from the "Clifford Avenue joint" (Social Club of Monroe), which was a gambling joint run by the mob.

According to Gina, "That's where the guys would go across the street, grab something to eat or have a cocktail or two, and even though they cooked in the joint, that's where my father used to take me. He'd go and have a cocktail and he'd get me a kiddy cocktail."

* A Special thank you to Ray Joseph for helping to identify some of the people in this photo.

A couple of years after the photo was taken, on June 10, 1978, a bomb exploded at the Clifford Avenue joint during the height of the Rochester Mob Wars, and another bomb was found (unexploded) outside of the Cozy Corner Bar by a young boy.

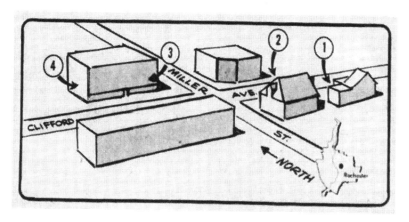

The Clifford Avenue joint (Social Club of Monroe) is at the top, left hand corner (3), and The Cozy Corner Bar is number (2) on the right.

Sam Gingello and Dick Marino
Meet Nixon Look Alike

On the left is Richard (Dick) Marino, in the center is a President Richard Nixon look alike, comedian James LaRoe, and on the right is Salvatore "Sammy G" Gingello. Unfortunately the date and location of this photo are unknown.

85

Chapter 3:

William Mahoney and
Operation Step-up (Set-up)

William Mahoney joined the Rochester Police force in 1952. By 1956 Mahoney had been promoted to detective. It wasn't long before William Mahoney began coming into contact with members of organized crime while working the streets of Rochester, N.Y. He participated in the arrest of "Charles J. (Babe Ruth) Blandino" on May 8, 1957. Blandino was charged with being a bookmaker. (1) Blandino's operation was later taken over by Abe Hamza, who regularly paid off the police to protect his operation.

On Feb. 1, 1968, Detective Bill Mahoney headed an investigation that led to a raid at Joe Lippa's Food Market, located at 82 Prospect St., where stolen merchandise as well as cash and betting slips were seized. Joe Lippa was known to be "the banker" for a large numbers operation. He had been arrested more than 30 times and claimed on several occasions to have had large amounts of cash stolen from him by the police. (2)

> Many times there were rumors of his close ties with the mob and an association in the restaurant business with gangster Billy Lupo, who later was slain.

Many times there had been rumors that William Mahoney had close ties to the Mob, and specifically an association in the restaurant business with gangster Billy Lupo. Mahoney socialized downtown and ate at the Rascal Café and Eddie's Chop House. He was there at Eddie's, on the fateful morning of April 23, 1978, just moments before Sammy Gingello's car exploded across the street. Perhaps a not so coincidental coincidence. (3)

Billy Lupo's death remained an unsolved homicide, but Sammy Gingello was considered by police to be a prime suspect. Gingello and Lupo were next door neighbors. Just prior to Lupo's death, Sammy Gingello reported the theft of $125,000 from his home. Police speculated that the robbery may be related to Lupo's death. Also, both men were members of the Rochester Mafia. Lupo was a Captain and Gingello a Soldier. After Lupo's death, Sam Gingello replaced Lupo as Captain in the "Organization."

In any event, the point is that William Mahoney had a very good motive for viciously and illegally pursuing criminal prosecutions of the remaining members of organized crime in general, and Sam Gingello in particular. If the rumors about Mahoney and Lupo being "business partners" were true, Mahoney would have suffered some kind of financial loss with Lupo's death. The blame for that financial loss would have laid directly with the other members of the Rochester Mob.

Coincidently, in **early 1974** William Lombard was elected Sheriff and he named William Mahoney as his chief of detectives. The prime directive, according to Lombard, was to pursue organized crime, and Mahoney would zealously work toward fulfilling that goal. If revenge was on his mind he would soon have the opportunity to get his. (4)

**William
Mahoney**

By the **end of that year (1974),** William Mahoney had contrived an elaborate master plan to bag some Mob guys; a plan he commonly referred to as "Operation Step-Up." But not even Mahoney could have predicted at the time "what a tangled web he'd weave" while fulfilling that plan.

Chief of Detectives William Mahoney Masterminds Stolen Property Scheme in order to Frame Mobsters

Francis J. Pecora

Francis J. Pecora was a professional shoplifter. According to his sworn testimony, he was ordered by Chief of Detectives William Mahoney to drive to Buffalo, N.Y. and shoplift some very specific items. He was then told to return to Rochester and sell those items to a known fence named Zeke Zimmerman.

Pecora testified that Chief of Detectives William Mahoney threatened him with jail time if he did not go to Buffalo and steal merchandise that was to be used to set up another booster named Jake Zimmermann. Pecora said that he had already signed a statement against Zimmerman, but that was not good enough for Mahoney.

The reason for Pecora's cooperation was simple. Francis Pecora had been charged with grand larceny on Aug. 16, 1974 after stealing $8,000 worth of diamond rings from Present Co. in Penfield on Aug. 7, 1974.

Then, in **December of 1974,** police were called to Pecora's home for a domestic disturbance and Pecora's wife began telling police about stolen guns and other stolen merchandise in the home. Pecora was taken to the Monroe County Jail where he managed to contact Chief of Detectives William Mahoney, whom he had known from previous encounters on the street and asked him for his help. "Bill, can you give me a break," Pecora asked.

Mahoney agreed to help Pecora. It was from this conversation that a deal was hatched between the two men. This was the origin of William Mahoney's masterplan, which he proudly referred to as "Operation Step-Up." (10)

Chief of Detectives William Mahoney

Mahoney's plan was to set up another booster named Zeke Zimmerman with the stolen goods that Francis Pecora acquired from the Buffalo shoplifting spree, and then wait until Zimmerman was in possession of the stolen goods. Once Zimmerman had possession of the goods, Mahoney would raid Zimmerman's house, arresting him. Pecora was given specific orders to make sure that each item was valued at more than $250, so felony possession of stolen property charges could be brought against Zimmerman.

Mahoney knew that Zimmerman would rat out his customers and hopefully some Mob guys rather than face jail time. Some of Zimmerman's customers were known to be members of the Rochester Mafia, which would allow police to arrest them for possession of stolen property. All of this was part of William Mahoney's masterplan. (5)

On **Dec. 19, 1974,** Francis Pecora completed his mission for Bill Mahoney. Upon returning home to Rochester from Buffalo with his car full of stolen goods, he stopped at the Leroy exit on the New York State Thruway at 3 p.m. and called Mahoney to inform him that he was on the way. Mahoney instructed Pecora to meet Detective Anthony Malsegna at the Churchville exit, which he did.

Malsegna led Pecora to a garage in Churchville where they hid the carload of stolen goods inside. Malsegna then drove Pecora to the detective's Bureau. From there, Pecora called Zimmerman and made plans to sell him the stolen goods at 7:30 p.m. that evening.

Anthony Malsegna

William "Zeke" Zimmerman was arrested that evening on **Dec. 19, 1974,** and immediately began telling police about Mob activity just as William Mahoney predicted he would. Mahoney's plan seemed to be working.

One of Zimmerman's first disclosures was that he sold a leather jacket that he had stolen from Sibley's in the Eastview Mall to Salvatore Gingello. The sale allegedly took place two months earlier, in October of 1974, outside of The Northway Social Club.

Both men, Francis Pecora and Zeke Zimmerman, ended up being housed together in a jail apartment. While incarcerated together, Pecora told Zimmerman how he was set up by Bill Mahoney. Zimmerman secretly tape recorded the conversation. The tape eventually made its way to the FBI via Albert DeCanzio, who turned informant against the Monroe County sheriff's office. (6)

William "Zeke" Zimmerman

Sammy Gingello Turns Himself In Following Raid

Based on the information provided by Zeke Zimmermann, police conducted a search warrant on **Dec. 29, 1974** at the residence of Sam Gingello. Sammy was out of town, in Miami, Florida when the warrant was served on an apartment that he maintained at 35 Portland Parkway, in Rochester, N.Y..

Police confiscated a camera, a movie projector, two leather coats and a tennis racket, all suspected of being stolen items. Police then issued a warrant for Gingello's arrest for possession of stolen property. Twelve other Rochester residents were arrested on the same charges following similar raids at their homes.

Sammy Gingello, on the left, and Samuel DiGaetano, his attorney.

Sam was informed of the warrant and he was met by his attorney, Samuel J. DiGaetano, at the airport upon his return to Rochester. He then promptly turned himself in to authorities. (7)

Accused Union Chief is Suspended from City Job

Anthony Gingello, Sammy's brother, was City Employee Union Local 1635 president. He was also one of the other 12 men arrested on **Dec. 29, 1974** and charged with possession of stolen property.

Police seized a leather coat and a pair of binoculars that they claimed were stolen property. As a result of his arrest on felony charges Gingello was suspended, without pay, from his job as a truck driver foreman as well as his position as union president.

Gingello, who was elected president of the union in 1970, had also just recently been named President of Council 66, New York State Council of public employees union.

Three months later, in March of 1975, Gingello was reinstated to his position following an Arbitration Hearing where the arbitrator ruled in his favor. All of the stolen property charges filed against him were eventually dropped. (8)

Dec. 31, 1974
Democrat and Chronicle

91

Miami, Florida - 11 years old - after Christmas
The Charge with the Booster
Models / Shopping

When we arrived in Miami, Florida we went directly to my father's home that he owned there. The next day he took us to the Diplomat Hotel to go swimming and have some lunch.

Models would walk around the Diplomat pool, modeling different outfits that you could purchase. So my father bought my cousin a beautiful outfit, resembling the ones jockeys wear. It was gorgeous. It came with a cute little cap and she looked stunning in it.

We went shopping, non-stop. I think he loved buying me clothes more than I did. I would have to model each outfit and he would choose which one he loved the most. I had a shopping spree every winter, spring, summer and fall, even down to matching coats, jackets, shoes and boots."

Grandma G., Grandpa G., my cousin, my father, Janice (mom), Joey Tiraborelli and myself had seen Frank Sinatra at the Diplomat on New Year's Eve. We went to the Diplomat Hotel almost every day to go swimming and sunning. The ocean and the beach were right there. But getting to see Frank Sinatra on New Year's Eve, WOW. We had dinner first, then out came Frank. What a night. We all had a wonderful time of course. It was just amazing."

During the time we spent in Florida we had dinner at one of dad's friend's home. His name was John (Tree Top) Imburgia. His wife made a lovely dinner for us. We felt very welcomed there and of course dad and Tree Top went into another room to talk about whatever as we finished dessert and then helped to clean up.

According to Gina Gingello, "We were in Florida and dad had to leave suddenly because of possession of stolen property charges filed against him after a booster back in Rochester, N.Y. began naming names of recipients of his goods."

It was nothing for me or my mom (Janice) to worry about. "Just take care of Gina," he said to my mom. That is what he always said to her.

So dad and Joey Tiraborrelli flew back to Rochester and the rest of us stayed in Miami another week. They had to go back home or the police would have come to Florida and brought him back.

Lawrence Masters

Lawrence Masters

A couple of weeks later, on **Jan. 16, 1975**, Jack Kinnicutt, the undersheriff of Monroe County, contacted Lawrence Masters under the auspices of discussing their friend William Lombard's political future. Masters was the former Manager of the Irondequoit Motor Vehicles office that was robbed in 1973.

But when Kinnicutt arrived, there was no friendly political discussion. Rather Kinnicutt immediately whisked Masters away and took him downtown for what would be a 20 hour interrogation session.

At that time, William Mahoney, who was the Chief of Detectives, then threatened to "hang Masters" with the 1973 robbery if he did not "cooperate."

Lawrence Masters was just one of 16 victims that eventually testified against William Mahoney at his conspiracy trial for civil rights violations. Masters said Mahoney pressured him into "cooperating" by threatening to blame him for the Irondequoit Department of Motor Vehicles robbery.

Masters testified that he never had anything to do with the robbery. Lawrence Masters spent more than one year in jail before his conviction was overturned and he was released. (11)

*****

Charles Monachino signed two affidavits, one on **March 8, 1975** and one on **March 10, 1976**. Both were filed in Henrietta Town Court.

Monachino's brother, Charles, who has been held in protective custody by sheriff's detectives, also signed two affidavits, one on March 8, the other March 10. Both are on file in Henrietta court.

*****

Sheriff Lombard Informed about the Buffalo Heist

On **March 19, 1975,** Francis Pecora informed Sheriff William Lombard that it was Chief of Detectives William Mahoney who had engineered the Buffalo heist. But Lombard did not believe him. In response, Pecora said that Lombard called him a "blundering fool." Lombard also denied any recollection of that conversation.

On **March 13, 1975,** at a preliminary hearing for the murder of William Constable, the charges against Al DeCanzio were dismissed as "hearsay evidence," and he was released.

Nicholas DeRosa

Detective Sgt. Nicholas DeRosa resigned from the sheriff's office after Zeke Zimmerman disclosed that he had given the officer two stolen suits in return for giving him a ride home.

DeRosa's **April 10, 1975** testimony also revealed that he was once asked by Zeke Zimmerman to deliver a message to Angelo Monachino. Zimmerman wanted Monachino to know that he was not the informant that ratted him out, and it was not his testimony that led to Monachino's arrest despite Monachino being arrested a mere eight hours after Zimmerman decided to cooperate with authorities. (12)

But Zimmerman's disclosures did lead to the arrest of Charles Monachino, who then fingered his brother Angelo Monachino. Both of the brothers then entered into the Federal Witness Protection Program and their revelations led to the arrest and prosecution of six men, alleged to be the hierarchy of the Rochester Mafia, for the 1973 murder of Vincent Massaro. (13)

D&C photo by Bob Gapsky

Shotgun-carrying police guard Charles Monachino, in light coat, witness in slaying case.

Police carrying shotguns guard Charles Monachino, pictured second from right, in the light jacket.

Al DeCanzio Convicted of Murder

Angelo Monachino was not the only "made" Mob guy that brother Charles Monachino fingered. Charles also gave police complete details of the 1973 Irondequoit Motor Vehicle robbery that ended with the murder of Ernest White. The murder was committed by Al DeCanzio, Charles Monachino's best friend. Charles had been Best Man at DeCanzio's wedding a few years prior.

Albert J. DeCanzio was also a Soldier in the Rochester

Charles Monachino's testimony led to the arrest of Angelo Monachino (left) and Al DeCanzio (right).

Mafia. On **May 15, 1975** he was convicted of murdering Ernest White, an accomplice in an armed robbery. Immediate following the execution style murder of White, who was tied up and put into a the trunk of a car, DeCanzio turned to his friend Charles Monachino and said, "This was number 16."

On **Aug. 8, 1975,** DeCanzio was sentenced to the minimum time possible for a murder conviction. He was given 15 to life due primarily to his cooperation with police concerning other crimes committed by the Rochester Mafia. (9)

Albert DeCanzio

Albert J. DeCanzio Jr.

In **May of 1975** Rochester Mafia Soldier, Albert DeCanzio, was convicted of murdering Ernest White, his accomplice in The 1973 Irondequoit DMV robbery. Within one week he became a police informant.

DeCanzio, 35, was convicted of murder in May 1975, and sentenced to 15 years to life in prison. He became a police informant about one week after his conviction, he said.

In August of 1975, DeCanzio was sentenced to 15 years to life. But as a result of his full cooperation with police, DeCanzio remained in the Monroe County Jail instead of being remanded to a regular prison facility. That way DeCanzio would be available to testify against local Mob figures he was ratting out. By his own admission, DeCanzio said he spent most of his time in the Monroe County Sheriff's Department, where he had access to a couple of offices including Bill Mahoney's office.

In a more startling disclosure, one of the defense attorneys claimed to have evidence that Albert DeCanzio and Angelo Monachino, both self admitted murderers, "walked around the sheriff's office with loaded firearms."

Turco said he also has evidence that Albert DeCanzio and Angelo Monachino, two reputed Mafia figures turned police informers, "walked around the sheriff's office with loaded firearms."

June 7, 1975
Angelo Monachino Tells Court of 'Our Thing'

Monachino tells court of 'Our Thing'

By THOM AKEMAN

Angelo Monachino talked matter-of-factly during a preliminary hearing in City Court yesterday afternoon about a secret organization from which he defected June 7.

"Many people call it many different things," he said. "They call it The Arm,' The Mob, 'Mafia,' 'Cosa Nostra.'

"I call it 'our thing.' It is our thing."

And that organization has "what they call the 'underboss. Technically, he's supposed to be second in command," Monachino testified. Monachino identified the underboss here as Salvatore "Sammy G" Gingello, 35, the head of Sampon Trucking Corp. and SJS Trucking Corp., both at 10 Woodward St.

It has "captains," one of whom he identified as Thomas E. Marotta, 33, of 471 Hazelwood Terr.

And it has "soldiers," one of whom he identified as Samuel 'Sammy Dig'' DiGaetano, 50, a Rochester criminal lawyer.

Those three members of that organization and Monachino had a meeting about 11 a.m. one weekday during the last week of April, Monachino said.

That meeting was held in the trucking companies' warehouse, in an inner office

Angelo Monachino
mob informer

Turn to Page 2B

On **June 7, 1975,** Angelo Monachino defected from the Rochester Mafia and became an informant. He had been facing jail time for other unrelated crimes when he decided to turn state's evidence. In great detail he began outlining for police the structure of the organization he belonged to. He identified the Underboss, Sam Gingello, a Captain, Thomas Marotta, and a Soldier, Samuel DiGaetano, who was also a Rochester criminal attorney.

On **June 18, 1975,** Monachino admitted to participating in the Massaro murder. He testified to participating in almost daily meetings where criminal activity was discussed, including the murder of Vincent "Jimmy The Hammer" Massaro in 1973. Monachino would be instrumental in helping police solve the Massaro murder case, which had been up until then classified as an unsolved homicide.

Monachino knew all the details of the murder as well as the participants. He happened to know those things because he was a willing participant to that crime.

Monachino's defection was the first of its kind (in Rochester), offering a first hand view into Rochester's organized crime scene. But it certainly would not be the last. Eventually more than 16 people from Rochester, along with their families, would enter into the Federal Witness Protection Program. (14)

Salvatore 'Sammy G' Gingello displays handcuffs as he arrives at Monroe County Jail for questioning shortly after break-out Town Court Justice dismissed stolen property charges against him
D&C photo by Steve Crien

Stolen property charge dropped against 'Sammy G' Gingello

On **June 26, 1975,** the possession of stolen property charge placed against Sammy Gingello was dismissed after the prosecution failed to give Gingello's defense attorney a copy of Zeke Zimmerman's grand jury testimony. Gingello had been charged with possessing an alleged stolen leather coat. (15)

Affidavit Signed by Angelo Monachino

On **July 1, 1975,** the Democrat and Chronicle newspaper ran a story that disclosed a very detailed affidavit signed by Angelo Monachino, a self admitted member of the Rochester Mafia.

Monachino made a number of startling claims including the fact that he was a member of an "Organization" sworn to secrecy in criminal activity. He disclosed that attorney Sam DiGaetano was another sworn member, adding that they were initiated on the same day at Frank Valenti's Ward Hill Road home in Henrietta, also nicknamed "The Farm." Monachino also said that Sammy Gingello was present that day.

Affidavit signed by Monachino

This is the affidavit signed by Angelo Monachino yesterday before the arrests of Samuel DiGaetano and Thomas Marotta on charges of conspiracy to murder Sheriff William Lombard and chief of detectives William Mahoney.

ANGELO MONACHINO, being duly sworn, deposes and says:

1. That he is a sworn member of an "Organization" the members of which are sworn to secrecy in criminal activity

2. That sometime in the month of April, 1975, your deponent was in attendance at a meeting of several members of said "Organization" at the offices of Sampon Trucking, 10 Woodward Street, Rochester, New York. Among those in attendance at said meeting was Thomas Marotta and Samuel DiGaetano, Esq. Your deponent knows that said DIGAETANO is a member of said "Organization" because your deponent was present when said DIGAETANO was "sworn into" the "Organization" at the farm of Frank Valenti on Ward Hill Road in the Town of Henrietta some time prior to said meeting. Salvatore Gingello was also present at said meeting

3. The purpose of said meeting was to discuss the pending criminal cases of certain members of the "Organization" following many recent arrests by the Monroe County Sheriff's Department.

4. During the meeting said GINGELLO stated that the time had come that some one should be "knocked down" (killed) in order to set an example

5. Your deponent then asked who could

Angelo Monachino

be hit to effectively set such an example

6. Said GINGELLO then suggested either Chief of Detectives William Mahoney or Sheriff William Lombard.

7. Said DIGAETANO then stated that was a very good idea and "Somebody better do something."

8. Said MAROTTA then stated that he knew where Sheriff Lombard goes bowling every week by himself and that "we've been watching him." MAROTTA further stated that the bowling hall was Brighton Bowl and that the parking area was like a dead end street

9. Said MAROTTA currently holds the title of "Captain" in said "Organiza-

Turn to Page 2A

99

Monachino named Thomas Marotta as a Captain of the Organization and claimed to have attended a meeting with Gingello, Marotta and DiGaetano at Sam-John Trucking Co., where Sam Gingello allegedly made the suggestion that either Sheriff William Lombard or Chief of Detectives William Mahoney should be killed as an example. He said Sam Gingello was the "Underboss" of the organization and DiGaetano was a "Soldier." (16)

Other disclosures were also made, and the arrests began.

Sam and Anthony Gingello among those Indicted for the Columbus Day Bombings (1970)

On **July 24, 1975,** Frank Valenti, Anthony Gingello, Sammy Gingello, Thomas Didio, Angelo Vaccaro, Dominic Celestino, Eugene DeFrancisco, and Rene Piccarreto were all indicted by a Federal Grand Jury on bomb charges in relation to the 1970 Columbus Day Bombing incident.

Frank Valenti had his case severed from the other defendants. In the end, Eugene DeFrancesco was the only one found guilty of the charges. He was sentenced to 11 years in prison. All the other defendants were found not guilty.

Anthony Gingello Loses His Union Post After Arrest

Within hours of his arrest, Anthony Gingello was again suspended from his position as President of Local 1635 of the American Federation of State, County, and Municipal Employees. In further action the international union placed Gingello's union in an emergency trusteeship. (17)

Gingello loses his union post after arrest

By JOHN McGINNIS

Anthony M. Gingello
handcuffed after arrest

Aug. 24, 1975
Fundraiser Dinner Held for Sammy G.

Gingello friends eat, drink, give $100,000

By THOM AKEMAN

More than 100 people attended a $500 a plate testimonial dinner yesterday for Salvatore (Sammy G) Gingello, Rochester reputed Mafia underboss.

The event started at 1 p.m. and lasted into the evening to help raise a legal defense fund for Gingello.

More than 100 additional guests joined the diners about midway in the banquet at 5 p.m., for a $100-a-ticket cocktail party.

The combined parties raised the $100,000 they were intended to raise, said one of the three men on the dinner committee, Joseph F. Tiraborelli.

The money will be used to hire famed criminal lawyer F. Lee Bailey to defend him, Gingello said.

Gingello, who faces 19 felony charges in Monroe County and federal courts, said he first learned of the dinner Wednesday, while talking to a newspaperman.

It was to have been a surprise party, Tiraborelli said.

Everyone who bought tickets to the dinner showed up at Amalfi's Restaurant, 1331 St. Paul St., Tiraborelli said.

Turn to Page 3B

On **Aug. 24, 1975,** more than 100 people attended a $500 per plate fundraising dinner in honor of Sammy Gingello. The dinner was held at Amalfi's Restaurant at 1331 St. Paul Blvd. in order to help raise funds for Gingello's legal defense. The dinner guests were joined by another 100 people who later paid $100 each for a cocktail party. Together, the events raised more than $100,000.

Sammy was facing 19 felony charges and intended to use money raised to hire famed criminal attorney F. Lee Bailey. (18)

Mob Captain Thomas Marotta and his third wife Mary arrive at a fundraiser dinner for "Underboss" Sammy Gingello's legal defense fund. (59)

Above is a photo of Sam taken at the fundraiser.

Knowing that the event would be a virtual who's who in the Rochester Mafia, newsmen and the police, not surprisingly, diligently staked out the party. The State Police were parked on Avenue D, directly across the street from the restaurant, and in an undercover van pretending to be from the New York Telephone Co. In addition to the state police, there were four Monroe County Sheriff detectives in an unmarked car watching the party goers. (18)

D&C photo by Steve Groe

Sheriff's Chief of Detectives William C. Mahoney
... Deputies and State Police watched outside banquet

Chief of Detectives William Mahoney (above) was seen driving by Sam Gingello's party.

With all the police and newsmen present and observing and recording the entire event, one would think that they had the situation pretty well covered. So it was rather curious that the Chief of Detectives, William Mahoney, was spotted making a personal appearance. Mahoney was a man who seemed to have a personal interest in the demise of not only the Mafia in general, but Sammy Gingello in particular.

'It's Getting Chilly Out and I Want My Coat Back'

Sam Gingello and Nick Fasco. Sammy is wearing the brown leather jacket that was seized by the Sheriff's Department.

Sammy Gingello's brown leather jacket was seized by the Monroe County Sherriff's Department during a raid on his Portland Parkway apartment on Dec. 29, 1974. Sam was one of a dozen alleged mobsters charged with possession of stolen property.

That charge was dropped months earlier on June 26, 1975 by Irondequoit Town Judge Michael J. Taddonio and now it was Fall, early **September of 1975,** and Sam wanted his jacket back. "I didn't think about it until it got chilly out," said Sam.

When the weather changed Gingello tried to get his coat back, but to no avail. Gingello said, "I called the sheriff's office to get the jacket and they told me they're appealing the case."

Detective Lt. John Kennerson, head of the sheriff's major crimes unit, said he explained to Gingello that the District attorney's office was holding the jacket for evidence.

While the possession of stolen property charge was dropped, Sammy had since been charged with 19 felony charges that included bombings, murder, and extortion. (19)

Prior to being set up for the Massaro murder, Salvatore Gingello did not have a felony police record. In fact, he had only been arrested a few times mostly for gambling. Nothing more than misdemeanor offenses.

Mahoney and Kennerson Lie About Confession

A special County Court hearing was held on **April 15, 1976** to determine whether or not a statement was made by Richard Marino to Sheriff's deputy John Kennerson and if so, could that statement be used at Marino's murder trial. Detective Kennerson testified that Dick Marino admitted to attending a meeting at 45 Longview Terrace on Nov. 23, 1973, the same day Vincent Massaro was murdered. According to Kennerson, Dick Marino named Rene Piccarreto, Samuel Russotti, Salvatore Gingello, Joseph Tiraborelli, Angelo Monachino, Eugene DiFrancesco and Joseph Lanovara as also attending the meeting where Massaro's murder was planned. Chief of Detectives, William C. Mahoney, then testified at the hearing, claiming that Marino told him all about the meeting on June 28, 1973, and named all attendees during an interview. Mahoney also claimed to have taken notes during the interview.

Arthur F. Turco, Richard Marino's lawyer, said that was an absolute lie. He was so sure that Mahoney was lying that he taunted him about his (Mahoney's) refusal to take a lie detector test. Turco also claimed that Mahoney's notes were fabricated as well. Those were outlandish claims, even for a defense attorney. Turco's defense rested on convincing the jury that the police had lied, and not just a couple of detectives, but the Chief of Police too. In the end the jury would believe the police. But as it would later be discovered, both the sheriff's deputies and Chief of Police Mahoney all lied and fabricated evidence that resulted in the imprisonment of five men, including Salvatore Gingello, for more than a year.

Richard Marino would be the first one to stand trial for the murder of Vincent "Jimmy The Hammer" Massaro. [20] On **June 23, 1976,** after a short trial and a mere six hours of jury deliberations, Richard Marino was found guilty of the Massaro murder. [21]

Checking on Dick Marino's Family

Dick was the first to go to jail. My dad would pick me up and we would drive over to Diane Marino's home. When we walked in, usually Diane would be in the kitchen and the girls (Marino children) would be in the living room.

Dad and I would say a general hello to everyone and then dad would go hug Susie, the youngest child. He would get down on his hands and knees and give Susie horsey back rides. While he was doing that he would talk to the oldest daughter, Leane. After a little while he would go into the kitchen and talk to Diane.

He would ask her if everything was okay with her and the kids, especially little Dicky. He would make sure that the kids were behaving themselves. And then he always gave Diane a stack of money. I never knew how much, but she would always smile and say Thank You. What a beautiful woman she was.

My father did the right thing for Dick and his family when Dick was away in jail. But the favor was NEVER RETURNED! After my father died, he (Dick Marino) never came and checked on me. He never brought my mother any money. Not even a phone call.

Tom Marotta was the only one who loved my father enough to always be there for me, even when he was in prison. When I gave birth to my first child, Angelo, Tom even found a way to have a beautiful bouquet of white and baby blue carnations sent to me and my baby. He would either write to me or call me from prison to check on not only me but my son Angelo also.

Tom was the only one that had the love and respect for my father to look after his family. He did what you are supposed to do, which is take care of each other. The others all turned their backs. A cousin on my mother's side was delivering sandwiches one day to where they were having a meeting. He overheard Dick Marino saying, "How much should we give for the kids," meaning my father's children. The response from Rene Piccarreto was, "Sam's kid's need no money and if I died I wouldn't expect my kids to receive any money." But the difference was that Rene's kids were grown adults and we were 14 and under.

The Trial

My father kept me involved in the trial as much as possible. The first day we drove to the courthouse in a limousine with F. Lee Baily and James Merberg, my fathers attorneys. It was of course a mob scene with all the reporters, cameras and TV crews.

Dad looked at me and said, "Are you ready?" The two attorneys got out first, then dad and me behind them. "You always keep your chin up. Look straight ahead and try not to make eye contact with anyone," is what my father said to me as we exited the limo. So that is what I did. I sat behind my father and the others and their attorneys. And so it began.

I wasn't able to go every single day. But when I did go, I will be honest, it was all very confusing to me. But dad always explained it to me in his own way so I could understand. And still there was much that made no sense. I mean how could you possibly positively identify a person from the distance of two to three football fields away. Yet that's what they did. As the trial lingered on, Baily left Merberg in charge.

My father never lied to me and I knew in my heart of hearts he was telling me the truth. He told me how he said to F. Lee Baily, "Everything is going to come out all right because my daughter told me, 'Daddy I know you're innocent.'"

Somehow these rotten son-of-a-bitches convinced the jury that they were telling the truth. But juries typically have a tendency to believe testimony from law enforcement over the testimony of the accused.

Even after the judge sentenced my father to 25 years to life I still believed in his innocence and I knew some how, some way, he was coming home. Dad told me, "Don't worry we are going to appeal this and the truth will come out, you believe me right?" "Of course I do daddy. I know you are innocent," I responded.

They were weak minded individuals that were coerced into telling lies and fabricating evidence. They had to be spineless with no moral compass or backbone of their own to allow themselves to be talked into committing such a heinous crime.

They fed the court spoonful's of malarkey and the judge and Jury just ate it up. It was shameful! They didn't just destroy me and my family's lives, they destroyed the lives of five other families, whose men who were also falsely charged with the crime.

Every single family went through the exact same thing I did. We were all robbed of our fathers. And they (the dirty cops) just went on with their own lives, enjoying their families like it was NOTHING. These were the people that were trusted with protecting our city and instead they were the ones committing the crimes.

Anthony Gingello Elected

Gingello elected

Anthony M Gingello, suspended president of the city employes union, was elected president of that union, Local 1635 of the American Federation of State, County and Municipal Employes, at a meeting last night at Marco Polo's Party House.

Gingello was suspended in early February after a hearing officer of the local's international union ruled that he had broken union laws.

Union Steward Anne Giambrone said last night that Gingello was unopposed in his bid for the post.

Anthony M. Gingello was experiencing his own problems that year, having been suspended from his job as president of the city employees union Local 1635 in early February of 1976 for allegedly breaking union laws. But fortuitously, on **Aug. 26, 1976,** there was an election to fill that position. Gingello ran unopposed for that position, regaining the presidency.

Massaro Murder Trial Starts for Five Defendants

In late **September of 1976,** the trial for Red Russotti, Rene Piccarreto, Salvatore Gingello, Thomas Marotta and Eugene DiFrancesco, the other men accused of the Massaro murder, began, lasting roughly five or six weeks.

The testimony used to convict Richard Marino was also used to convict the other five men accused of murder and conspiracy. There were two prosecution witnesses, Angelo Monachino and Spike Lanovera, who outlined the entire conspiracy from the planning stage to the execution of the crime. Both men were made members of the Rochester Mafia who witnessed the crime. But they were also participants to that crime.

Their testimony was backed up with police detectives who staged an elaborate charade, faking surveillance notes and giving false testimony in order to gain convictions. (22)

Massaro Trial Jury Visits Alleged Stake-out Site

Defense lawyers Harold J. Boreanaz (left) and F. lee Bailey at the scene of the alleged police stakeout at 45 Longview Terrace.

On **Oct. 20, 1976**, trial participants including jurors in the Massaro murder trial, were taken to a home on Longview Terrace to view a home where the conspiracy plot to kill Vincent Massaro was allegedly hatched.

Two Monroe County Sherriff's Deputies testified to conducting surveillance at the home on Nov. 23, 1973. They claimed to have seen four of the six murder suspects, including Sammy Gingello, in the vicinity of the house that evening. Vincent Massaro was murdered shortly after the meeting ended.

In question at the time was whether or not the detectives could identify the suspects from a distance of 300 feet, where the alleged surveillance supposedly took place. Defense Attorney, F. Lee Baily drilled the detectives about specific features of each suspect that allowed them to positively identify the suspects. The intended point the defense was attempting to make was that no specific features could actually be identified from that range.

The real problem was that there was no actual police surveillance on the Longview Terrace home that evening. It was all lies. And the testimony provided by both Sherriff's deputies was fabricated, but necessary to secure convictions. (23) Unfortunately these facts would not be known until Sammy Gingello and his codefendants had already served more than 15 months in prison.

Sammy Gingello produced two alibi witnesses to back up his claim that he was in Miami, Florida on the date that the last conspiracy meeting, and the murder itself, allegedly took place. But police were able to find five witnesses of their own, all police officers, that claimed to have seen Sam around local Rochester gambling joints on the same day.

In the end the remaining five men charged, including Salvatore Gingello, would all be convicted.

According to police and the newspapers, Salvatore Gingello was the reputed Underboss of the Rochester Mafia. But according to Sammy he was just a trucking executive. Gingello owned Sam-John Trucking Inc. Prior to his conviction on **Nov. 10, 1976,** Sam had never been convicted of a felony. His entire "criminal history" consisted of five minor misdemeanor offenses mostly for gambling.

The newspaper pointed out that Sam maintained and lived at two different locations, the house on Plank Road where his mother lived and an apartment at 35 Portland Parkway. The paper also disclosed that Sam was twice divorced. But the paper failed to report any of the good things about Sam, like the fact that Sam looked after and provided for his brother Jim's children after Jim passed away.

Picture of Sam in his kitchen on Plank Road. Photo taken by Sam's daughter Gina in 1975 or 1976. Sam was about 36 years old.

But if one were to judge by photos of Sam taken during this time period, like the one on the left taken by his daughter Gina, you would never know the extent of Sam's real problems. He always displayed that contagious smile, even in the face of adversity. (24)

Chapter 4:

Police Conspiracy Against the Mob Produces Convictions

Five Guilty in Massaro Murder

On **Nov. 10, 1976,** all five men charged with the Massaro murder were found guilty. Each of the men faced life in jail. Outside the courtroom, despite facing a lengthy prison sentence, Salvatore Gingello was all smiles and hammed it up for photographers. (25)

His demeanor after the trial was strikingly similar to the photo taken by Gina (below) prior to the trial.

Cops Celebrate Convictions in Massaro Case

Nov. 10, 1976 District Attorney Lawrence Kurlander, who defeated Jack Lazarus in 1975, holds a newspaper during a victory party after convictions were announced in the Massaro murder case.

That same day, District Attorney Lawrence Kurlander, center, holds a newspaper during a victory party on **Nov. 10, 1976,** celebrating the convictions of all defendants charged with the murder of Vincent "Jimmy The Hammer" Massaro. (72)

The police and prosecution gathered at Earl's Grill, one of the few Third Ward taverns to survive urban renewal, and toasted their good fortune.

When Cornelius walked through the door of the back room where the celebration was being held, his colleagues greeted him, glasses raised, by humming a few bars of the theme from the movie "The Godfather."

One of the celebrants was informer Angelo Monachino.

On **Jan. 14, 1977,** Salvatore Gingello, 37, and the four other men, falsely convicted of the 1973 Jimmy "The Hammer" Massaro murder, were sentenced to lengthy prison sentences. Samuel "Red" Russotti, 63, Rene Piccarreto, 52, and Gene DiFrancesco were all sentenced to 25 years to life and Thomas Marotta, 34, received a lesser penalty of 15 years due to the prosecution failure to prove he was present at the second meeting, where Massaro's death was allegedly plotted.

Three of the men - Rene Piccarreto, Thomas Marotta and Eugene DiFrancesco, were taken to Attica Prison. (26)

Rene Piccarreto (second from left), Thomas Marotta, and Eugene DiFrancesco arrive at Attica State Prison to begin lengthy prison sentences.

Gina visits her father, Sam Gingello, at Attica State Prison.

The other two men convicted of the Massaro murder, Sammy Gingello and Samuel "Red" Russotti, were both originally sent to Dannemora Prison.

According to Sam's daughter Gina, the conditions inside the prison were so bad that Sam made Gina sit in the car in the parking lot when she visited. Sam did not want his daughter to see the horrific living conditions inside.

Later, Sam was sent to Attica prison where the photo (left) with his daughter Gina was taken.

The Password

Before my father went to prison, he and my mother sat me down and gave me a password. That if any person, even if I knew them, tried to get me to go with them, I was to refuse unless they knew "the password."

So one day I was walking home from Saint Philip Neri School with my friends. My Aunt Mickey (my father's sister) pulled up and told me to get in. "I am going to your house," she said. I asked her what the "password" was. She did not understand, so I had to tell her that if she didn't know the password I couldn't get in the car. She understood then and when I got home aunt Mickey's car was in the driveway.

Dad knew I enjoyed walking home with the rest of the kids in the neighborhood. So we came up with a password. But I also believe I wasn't really ever walking with just the kids in the neighborhood. I am sure he had someone watching out for me.

While Dad Was In Prison

When they first went to prison, Tom Didio would come to my home at 6 Manitou St. and would give my mother $50. From $50 it went to $25. Then one day he went to go hand her $20 and my mother told him, "Keep it, apparently you need it more than we do."

Shortly after that I ran into him at Fay's Drug store on Waring Road in Waring Plaza. The few things I had in my hands he insisted on buying. When I told my mother, I could tell she was upset. She told me to NEVER except anything from him, or anyone else, ever again!

Letters From Prison

When Sam Gingello went to prison he stayed in contact with his family as much as possible, especially his daughter Gina. Sam regularly wrote letters to Gina, who certainly looked forward to receiving them. Here are a few of those letters, including several originals written in Sam's own handwriting.

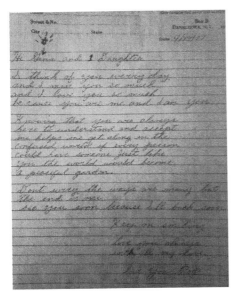

Dannemora, N.Y. 12929
4-18-77

Hi Gina and 1 Daughter,

I think of you every day and I miss you so much and I love you so much because you are me and I am you.

Knowing that you are always here to understand and accept me helps me get along in the confused world; if every person could have someone just like you, the world would become a peaceful garden.

Don't worry the ways are many but the end is one, see you soon because I'll (be) back soon.

Keep on smiling
Love you always
With all my love
Love you Pop

June 18, 1977 Father's Day

Shown below is the telegram I sent my dad to wish him a Happy Father's Day when he was in prison.

Letters From Prison

7-18-77

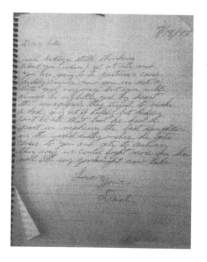

Dear babe,

Well daddy's still thinking about you, when I get out me and you are going to be partners cause daddy knows now you are not a little girl anymore but you will always be my little girl my heart. The newspapers, they tried to make a bad guy out of daddy, but daddy can't be all that bad, he had part in making the best daughter in the world daddy wishes he gets closer to you and gets to Auburn that way we could fight more ha ha well I'll say goodnight now babe.

8/1/77

Hi Babe

Daddy misses you where have you been. I have missed you a lot. When I see you I am going to punch you in the nose but you know I still love you. But Daddy still wants to see you. I think of you every day but I am still going to punch you in the nose. But you know you are still my baby and daddy is so proud of you. You are my whole life.

Love You Always

Your Pop

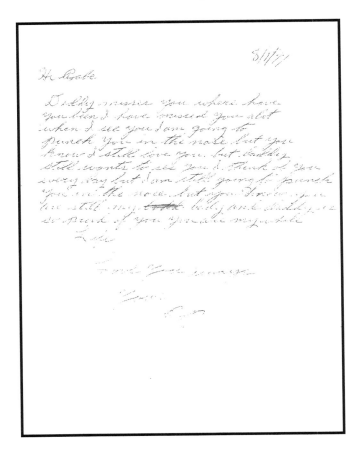

Hi ya babe And #1 Daughter,

Daddy was so happy to see you when I see you and talk to you I forget I am in prison, daddy dreams of the day he gets out to be with you and Sammy again I am so proud of the way you grew up I wish your brother takes after you. Keep on being a good person that you are but never let your heart get in the way of your brain always keep your eyes open. Daddy made the mistake of having a big heart he should have payed attention to his brain Don't worry about daddy cause daddy will be alright a girl that worries is a girl that gets cheated out of happiness so please don't worry and be happy.

Love You always,

You are my Life

Love Pop xoxo

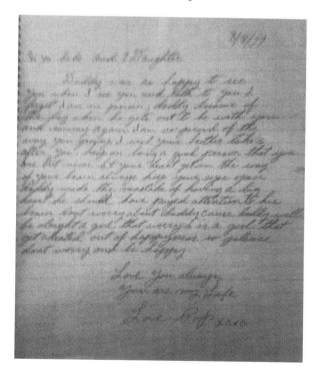

Hello Babe

Did Daddy ever tell you how much he loves you. Well if I did I am going to tell you again. You are my little sweetheart and you are my big sweetheart. Daddy was happy to see you. When I see you I forget where I am at. I hope soon we will be together but only God could say when. I hope he hurries up. Give him a call for me. I hope you like school when you go back. I hope you get all "A's" in your marks cause daddy used to get all "A's" for lunch hour, "A" for skipping school and an "A" for being in the most fights. (Ha Ha) Keep being the good girl that you are. Well goodnight babe say hello to my big sister and let me know if she gets any taller. (Ha Ha)

Love Always,

Your Pop

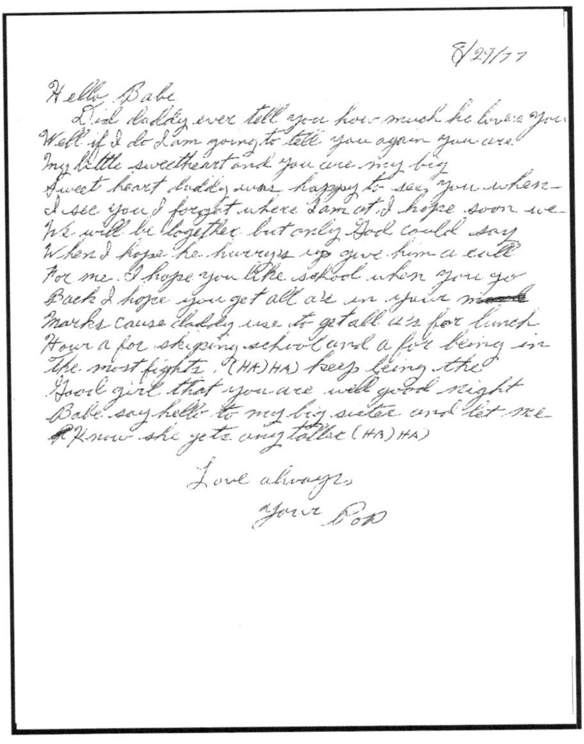

Dear Baby

You are my little puppy, daddy was so proud of the poems you sent me. I showed them to a few guys. I am the richest man in the world because I have your love. I miss you a lot baby. I hope to be with you soon and if they don't let me out of here soon I am going to get a sledge hammer and knock the wall down so I can be with my puppy. Tell your mother thank you for the card and tell her not to go to Florida cause the waves are too high and her legs are too short but she is still my Big sister.

Love you Always Your Pop xoxo

> Don't worry.
> The ways are many but
> the end is one.

> See you soon because
> I'll be back soon.
> Keep on smiling. Look at me.

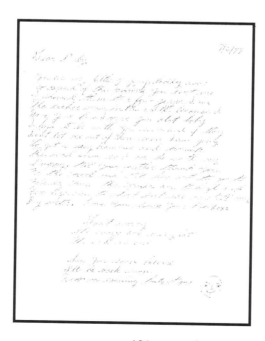

121

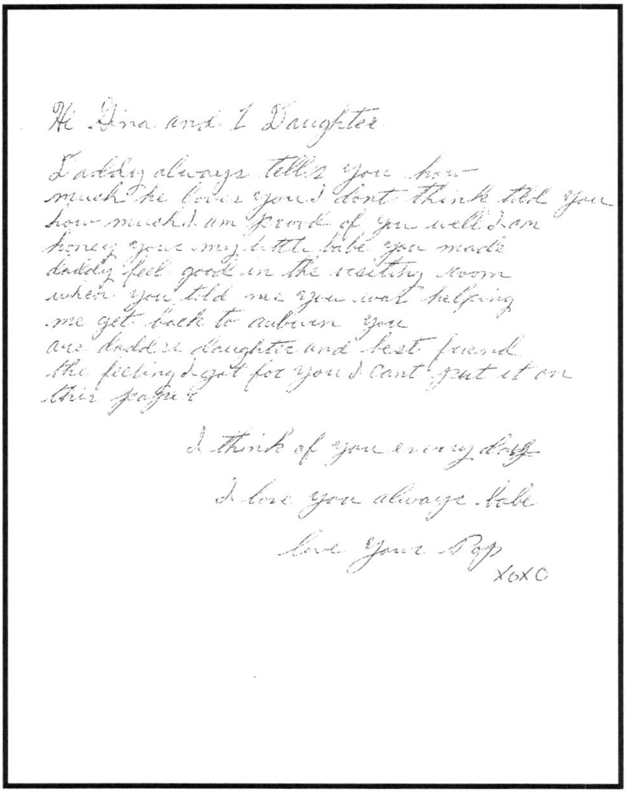

Hi Gina and 1 Daughter

Daddy always tells you how much he loves you. I don't think I told you how much I am proud of you well I am honey you are my little babe you made daddy feel good in the visiting room when you told me you was helping me get back to Auburn. You are daddy's daughter and best friend. The feeling I got for you I can't put it on this paper.

I think of you every day

I love you always babe

Love Your Pop xoxo

The Machiavellian Philosophy

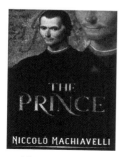

Above is a copy of the book "The Prince," by Niccolo' Machiavelli.

When my father was in prison he told me to read the book titled "The Prince." I tried really hard, but I did not understand it. But as I grew older I revisited the book and started to understand why he wanted me to read it.

When he went to prison and after he came home he used to tell me, "Never think with your heart always think with your head because daddy listened to his heart instead of his head and look where it got me." Machiavelli wrote:

"It is better to be feared than loved."

My father was a kind compassionate Big hearted person and wore his heart on his sleeve. A lot of people loved and respected my father. And that was enough for him, but I do believe after everything that happened to him he realized that respecting him was nothing compared to fearing him. That might be the reason why he got mad at Tom Taylor and Tom Torpey (his two bodyguards) for trying to check under his car (for bombs) and told them, "If anyone is watching it shows a sign of weakness."

Not by any means was my father weak, but I don't believe he was going to wear his heart on his sleeve anymore. Let me further explain, "Sonny" Celestino was fooling around with somebody's wife. That is a big NO NO within the "Organization." He should have been killed, but instead my father put him "on the shelf." That means he could no longer go to the gambling joints or associate with anyone within the organization. He spared his life when he should have taken it from him. And by my father sparing Celestino's life, Celestino in return took his!

Auburn Prison 1977

Standing, left to right, are Joe LaDolce, Dick (Fubb) Fabrizi, Sam Gingello, Charlie Russo, and Tom Marotta. Seated is Joseph (Snuffy) Grock. Only Sammy Gingello and Tom Marotta were actually in prison. The rest of the boys were visiting.

Going From Prison To Prison

He was first transferred to the Buffalo Jail. I couldn't go inside to see him there so I stayed in the car. I remember how gloomy, dreary, and rainy it was. After that he was moved to Dannemora Clinton Correctional Facility, which was 277.5 miles away from home. Then he went to Attica Prison, which is 48.6 miles away and took about 56 minutes to get there. Then Auburn Prison at 62.2 miles and Comstock, which was 259.2 miles away. It took four hours and 24 minutes to get there. That was each way.

My dad was so proud of me when I told him that I had written several letters to then Governor Mario Cuomo to try to get him transferred back to Auburn Prison from Comstock. But it never did happen. So just about every weekend was dedicated to going to see my father.

My Uncle Ted, my father's brother-in-law, would drive Grandma Gingello and myself from prison to prison. The trips grew further away as the months went on. And as the months went on the thinner dad looked. But when we were there to visit him he would always come out with the biggest smile on his face and his arms wide open, except for this one day.

On previous visits dad had told us about this one young guy who did not belong in there (Comstock). He was having a tough time and was very depressed. My dad felt bad for the guy and was trying to look out for him, but he could only do so much. As hard as my dad tried to help this guy he ended up killing himself. My dad was very upset about that. And I felt bad for my father because he genuinely cared for that kid.

Throughout all of the prison visits there was always one thing that pissed me off every time. If someone had arrived before us we would have to share the visiting time with them. I became very possessive of my time with my father and the only ones I was willing to share it with was Grandma Gingello and my Uncle Ted.

It was tough to give up almost every weekend as a young teenager. I could never make plans to do anything else because we would leave in the early morning hours, and by the time I got home I was tired from the ride and sad that I had to leave him.

Auburn Prison Summer 1977

In the bottom row Sam Gingello is in the center, and Red Russotti is the second from the right.

From the left are, John (Vac) Vaccerella, Thomas Marotta, Red Russotti, Uncle Boots, and Sam Gingello is at the far right.

Sammy the Artist

A little unknown fact about Sam Gingello was his artistic abilities. When he was younger he won a number of awards for his artwork. While imprisoned for 14 months, for the Massaro murder, Sam clung to the things he cherished most, which were memories of his family.

Using one of the few photos he had of his beloved daughter Gina, he drew his own portrait of her while passing the time in prison.

Photo of Gina Gingello that Sam carried with him in prison.

Portrait of Gina Gingello, drawn by her father Sam.

The Raid on 6 Manitou Street

During the time my father was in prison, my Grandpa Gennell, my mother's father, was left in charge of what was left of the Gas Station/Garage on Bay Street. By that time there was only a handful of trucks left and John (Flap) Trivigno was there with Grandpa.

I was in the eighth grade at St. Philip Neri School. So one day Stephanie Gangarosa came to pick me up from school, which was strange. I asked her where my mother was. She said, "There's something going on at the house. The cops are there."

We pulled down Manitou Street. "OH MY GOD!" The house at 6 Manitou St. was completely surrounded by marked police cars and undercover cars. The screen door on the front porch was propped open. The officers coming in and out of the front door were the ones flipping the house. The side screen door also was propped open near the driveway. And those officers focused only on the basement!

I walked in the front door and the whole house was flipped. They had my mother in the kitchen, questioning her. They kept on asking her where the scale and measuring spoons were. She told them the scale was in the bathroom and the measuring spoons were in the kitchen drawer. She was clueless. And they finally realized that.

Then one undercover cop goes to answer the house phone and I went off. "Who the Fuck do you think you are," I barked at him. Then I asked to see the search warrant. One cop, of course, was an asshole. But the other cop handed it to me. I didn't even know what it said. But in between all the mumbo-jumbo I saw the word "NARCOTICS."

The cops kept going into the basement. There was an old wine cellar with a huge wooden door and there was a lot of wood in there. I felt so bad for my mother. She didn't know what was going on. I was screaming and yelling at the cops, telling them to leave her (my mother) alone. "She doesn't know what you're talking about," I tried to explain. The whole time I was thinking that someone had done this to get back at my father.

Another phone call came in and they said, "Tell him we are taking his daughter downtown." And then they hung up. Not even a minute later a majority of the cops ran downstairs. They had found what they were looking for, DRUGS that my Grandpa Gennell had stashed in our basement.

Meanwhile down the street at 12 Manitou, they were also raiding my grandparents home but they didn't find anything there. They did arrest my uncle, my mother's brother, and they took my mother downtown too. So there I sat in a house torn apart by the cops. My mother was taken out. My uncle, my grandfather and my dad were already in jail. Of course, I looked around and started crying. I was there all by myself. I started to try to clean up. I was thinking, if my father was here this would have never happened.

My mother came home several hours later. So did my uncle. My grandfather served a year. My father was so pissed, and that is an understatement. Chief of Detectives William Mahoney, Detective John Kennerson, Assistant District Attorneys Brophy and Marks, and all the other cops that lied and fabricated evidence are responsible for setting all these things in motion.

Had the cops been honorable and did not lie or fabricate evidence, my father would have never went to prison. My grandfather would have NEVER did what he did. I wouldn't have had my childhood taken away from me. My children would have a papa (grandfather) and my grandchildren would have had a Great Papa (great-grandfather).

All that was never to happen because of a web of lies and deceit conceived by Rochester's finest, the police. I can only hope through the years that it came back on them, tenfold.

In **August of 1977,** Al DeCanzio petitioned then Governor Carey for executive clemency. If granted, DeCanzio would be freed from jail and would enter into the Federal Witness Protection Program, which he did, joining the Monachino brothers. (66)

DeCanzio was taken into Federal custody on Sept. 18, 1977. That is when the FBI began an investigation into the violations of civil rights of the suspects processed through the sheriff's department.

One early disclosure made by Albert DeCanzio was the fact that during the first three weeks of June 1977 DeCanzio was operating a bulldozer on William Mahoney's property, while he was supposed to be in jail. Mahoney attempted to get DeCanzio to sign an affidavit saying he never did the work, but DeCanzio refused to sign it.

As a result of the disclosure, Chief of Detectives William Mahoney was suspended from his job on **Sept. 22, 1977.** (67)

Albert DeCanzio
. . . 'won't sign anything illegal'

'Mahoney asked me to lie about bulldozer'

By JIM ROWLEY
D&C Staff Writer

Albert J. DeCanzio Jr., a convicted murderer, says William C. Mahoney, the suspended Monroe County sheriff's Chief of Detectives, asked him to sign an affidavit last July stating that he didn't drive a bulldozer behind Mahoney's house.

DeCanzio said he refused to sign the affidavit because it wouldn't be true. "I will not sign anything that's illegal," DeCanzio said, recalling what he told Mahoney. "I'm trying to rehabilitate myself."

When asked about DeCanzio's accu-

sations, Mahoney said he would have no comment. "I'm going to let him stick his neck out," Mahoney said.

Mahoney was suspended Sept. 22 by Monroe County Sheriff William M Lombard after he admitted that DeCanzio had done excavation work to stop erosion on his property during the first three weeks of June.

DeCanzio, 35, became a police informant after his May 1975 murder conviction. He was a special prisoner in the Monroe County Jail, until taken into federal custody Sept. 18. That is when the FBI began its civil rights

Turn to Page 3A

Oct. 30, 1977 Democrat and Chronicle Rochester, N.Y.

Mahoney, Kennerson Charged

Seven men, including five detectives, were indicted on April 12, 1979 by a federal grand jury that had been investigating corruption in the Monroe County Sheriff's office. Former Chief of Detectives, William Mahoney; former detective, Joseph Robortella; former detective, John Kennerson; former sheriff's polygraph operator Dennis Marinich; and Reginald Hawkins, a witness for the sheriff's department in two major trials were all indicted on five counts of conspiracy to injure, oppress, threaten, and intimidate 14 men.

John Kennerson   Joseph Robortella   Clayton Berardi

**Three former sheriff's detectives charged
with violating the civil rights of 14 men.**

Two men, Detective Clayton Berardi, and a man called William Tomkins, who was also known as William Sterling, were indicted for perjury. The second man was also a witness for the sheriff's department.

The indictment specifically listed 122 overt acts beginning Dec. 11, 1974 and ending Dec. 12 1977, violating the constitutional rights of 14 men. It was Al DeCanzio who first went to the federal authorities (FBI) in August of 1976 with accusations of widespread corruption within the sheriff's department. DeCanzio was able to accumulate a large amount of evidence for the FBI while he was incarcerated due to the freedom he enjoyed at the jail, which included access to Mahoney's office. (73)

Angelo Monachino   **Charlie Monachino**

Ange and Charlie

The Monachinos sang for freedom

By NANCY MONAGHAN
D&C Staff Writer

Together, Angelo and Charles Monachino received immunity for three murders, eight arsons, one robbery, five bombings and an array of stolen property charges.

Some of the men they testified against went to prison. Only one is still in jail.

Prosecutors and defense lawyers coined new phrases for the juries.

"We can't choose our witnesses," the prosecutors would say, after defense lawyers made sure jurors knew the Monachinos were arsonists, murderers and thieves.

"You're in the murder and extortion and stealing business?" one lawyer asked Charles Monachino in a robbery trial.

The Monachino brothers, Angelo and Charles, both entered into the Federal Witness Protection Program.

In all, Charles and Angelo Monachino received immunity for three murders, eight arsons, one robbery, five bombings, and an array of stolen property charges.

Angelo Monachino first admitted to killing two men, William Constable in 1970 and Vincent "Jimmy The Hammer" Massaro in 1973. He then told police that he would tell them more if he was granted immunity.

Together the brothers testified against 18 men in at least eight separate trials. Charles Monachino was a collector for Mafia Soldier and loan shark Eugene DeFrancesco. He worked on construction projects and admitted to stealing from all of them. He also admitted to helping dump a body down a storm sewer one time.

But surprisingly, the Monachino brothers had only been convicted of one crime between the both of them. Angelo was convicted of tax evasion prior to becoming an informant. (74)

Chapter 5:
Conspiracy Plot Exposed and
Massaro Murder Convictions are Reversed
Sammy Gingello is Freed From Prison

On **Jan. 31, 1978,** after serving roughly 15 months in prison, Sammy Gingello and his co-defendants were set free after discovering that the testimony used to convict them at their trials was fabricated.

Rita Piccarreto (right) embraces Gina Gingello, 14, following the release of Sammy Gingello (Gina's dad) and Rene Piccarreto.

William Marks, a former Sheriff's Investigator, testified to fabricating surveillance notes and falsely testifying at two trials, which resulted in the imprisonment of Gingello and four others. At the hearing, Marks testified that his 1976 testimony was "All a total lie - fabricated totally and completely." Marks had plead guilty to a felony charge of conspiracy to fabricate evidence.

Andrea Russotti at the court proceedings, awaiting her father's release.

After five hours of testimony, the bitterness felt by the family members of the men falsely imprisoned slowly gave way to tears of joy when the legal paperwork was produced by the district attorney's office and taken to judges for signatures, ordering the release of Sammy Gingello and Rene Piccarreto. The other men falsely convicted were being held at other prisons and were eventually released later that day. (47)

Dad is Released

Finally the day came and he was coming home. All of my prayers and Novenas had been answered. A Novena is a prayer using the Rosary. I prayed to God, Jesus, and St. Jude. I always knew my father was telling me the truth. When I first discovered that John Kenerson couldn't live with his conscience any longer and came clean, all I could think about was my father coming home. At first I was more excited about that than I was mad about discovering all the lies and fabricated evidence the police presented at the trial.

But eventually I couldn't help wondering how people could purposely ruin someone else's life and then continue on with their own lives with their families. My family had been torn apart. They got to enjoy their weekends and celebrate birthdays, holidays and have cookouts, and everything thing else. Well my weekends were spent driving from prison to prison with my grandmother and my uncle. I spent most of the time in the car going back and forth, just to enjoy a few precious hours with my father. The rest of the time I spent writing letters to help free my dad.

During the week I was afraid to go anywhere with my friends because I never wanted to chance missing one of my father's phone calls. On Father's Day I had to send my father a telegram instead of having dinner with him. When I went to my first Formal (school dance) I sent my dad a picture of myself instead of him being there with me. It's not the same to hear how beautiful you looked instead of hearing how beautiful you are.

They took my father from me. They stole my childhood. They ruined his life and my life all because they lied. The lies and fabrications that led to prison time for my father and his friends also needlessly upset the balance of power in Rochester's underworld and set in motion everything that came afterwards, including the bloody Mob Wars that followed.

Coming Home

Then the day finally came after the truth came out. HE WAS COMING HOME! I never did believe what was being said about my father. I only believed my dad. He told me from the beginning it was all lies.

Salvatore Gingello (right) and his attorney, James Merberg

Salvatore Gingello (right) and his attorney James Merberg. (85)

I remember standing outside of the Americana Hotel on State Street with my father and his attorney, James Merberg. Dad looked so thin. His suit looked a little big for him. But the look in his eyes was very readable. He looked relieved and happy. And when he looked at me I saw love lots and lots of love. I remember we held each other so tight. And I was breathing him in. He kept on kissing the top of my head.

Now it was time to go and let the celebration begin. There was a sea of people. Everyone was so happy and it was certainly a well deserved celebration at that. I sat at a two chair cocktail table and just watched him finally enjoy himself. He would glance over at me with that beautiful smile of his from time to time, just to see if I was okay. And I was. I didn't mind sharing him at all that night because we had the rest of our lives together, or so I thought.

Celebrating at "Red" Russotti's House

This picture was taken at Samuel "Red" Russoti's house following Sammy Gingello and Red's release from prison. Standing, top left, is Ida Russotti, wife of Red Russotti, Sammy Gingello on the right, and Red Russotti seated on the right at his kitchen table.

B-Team Plans to Kill Sammy Gingello

But there were already plans in motion by B-Team members to murder Sammy Gingello. After the release of the A-Team hierarchy from prison, almost daily meetings were conducted by B-Team members in Rochester, N.Y. Present at these meetings were B-Team members Thomas DiDio, Angelo Vaccaro, Dominic "Sonny" Celestino, Rosario "Ross" Chirico, William Barton, Frank Frassetto, and Rodney Starkweather.

It was at these meetings that that the decision was made to kill Salvatore "Sammy G" Gingello. Gingello was selected for the following reasons:

A) Frank Valenti was upset that Gingello was one of the individuals that forced him into retirement in 1972.

B) Thomas Didio and Stanley Valenti were aware that although relatively new as an Underboss, Gingello had successfully succeeded in uniting various factions within the organization. As a result of his personality and his generosity to his underlings, Gingello commanded the loyalty of his subordinates. The untimely death of Gingello would cause dissention within the ranks of the A-Team.

C) Due to Gingello's role as the top mobster in the City of Rochester, N.Y., killing him would most impress upon the gamblers and operators of illicit enterprises the courage and determination of the B-Team faction to retain control of the Organization.

D) Individually, many of the B-Team members had personal motives for seeking the death of Salvatore "Sammy G" Gingello. Rosario "Ross" Chirico, was the brother of Dominic Chirico, who was killed at the direction of Gingello in 1972. Anthony Chirico, the son of Rosario Chirico, was the nephew of Dominic Chirico. Angelo Vaccaro sponsored both Dominic and Rosario Chirico upon their entry into the Organization, and had strong personal ties to both men. At the direction of Gingello, Dominic "Sonny" Celestino had been beaten and ejected from the Mob in 1974 and was not allowed back into the Organization until Thomas Didio assumed control.

(page 442-443 1978 Senate Hearing)

Sometime between
Jan. 30, 1978 and April 23, 1978
The Talk About Drugs

I remember I was with him one day at his apartment at Portland Parkway. Dad had two residences, his apartment on Portland Avenue and his home on Plank Road, where his mother Angelina (Angie) Gingello lived with his brother Jim Junior's two oldest children, whom he had cared for since his brother passed away.

Dad not only cared for them, he made sure that they, along with Grandma Gingello, had the best of everything - cars, clothes, and money. They wanted for nothing and it made my dad very happy that he could do that for them.

He loved taking care of his family, all of us. None of us went without; nieces, nephews, sister, brother-in-law, sister-in-law. He loved taking care of all of us. If someone was in need of something, anything, dad was right there to provide for them and it made my dad very happy to be able to do so.

So anyway me and my cousin Tony were hanging out with my father at my Dad's apartment. Tony sat in the French Provincial chair near the window and my dad asked me to lie down next to him on the couch. He then proceeded to talk to the both of us about never doing drugs. As he held me in his arms he said, "DOPE IS FOR DOPES. And don't ever do drugs, because they are bad for you. Understand?"

We both said yes. He kissed me on my forehead and said, "Okay, let's go eat." I have to be honest and say my cousin Tony listened to my father. As for myself, after my father was murdered I was a rebel without a cause. At that point in my life, at 14 years old, I was lost. I drank and smoked pot, because I had no guidance by a parent.

There was a police officer who would not identify himself that once said, "All hell has broken loose. The police force should have protected Sam Gingello because now there is a drug war in the streets and he (Sam) had kept a handle on things." The officer knew that my father was responsible for keeping drug dealing to a minimum in the city due to his personal opposition to making money by destroying families and getting children hooked on drugs. Unfortunately that is a story we hear about every day now.

The Car Ride

My dad came to pick me up as usual. He pulled into the driveway at 6 Manitou St. with John Fiorino. John went to get out of the passenger seat so that I could sit next to my dad. And for the first time ever my dad told John, "No, I want Gina in the back seat."

Neither of us questioned him (dad). John opened the back door for me and I got in. He went and got back into the front passenger seat. Dad turned around smiled at me and tapped me on my leg as if trying to convey to me that everything was okay. But I knew then, with all the talk going on, which I was catching bits and pieces of, that there were people that liked my dad and there were people who didn't.

Lucky Star Vending

The company office for Lucky Star Vending was located on East Ridge Road. One day my dad received a phone call from his secretary, Rosie Wolskij, who told him that there was some guy walking around the building. My father told her to lock the door and he would be right there.

We pull up, and in between the driver and passenger seat in a cloth case was a sawed-off shotgun. He pulled it out, told me to get out of the car and stay close to his back. We went to the door and dad pounded on it, yelling for Rosie to open the door. Rosie opened the door, I went inside, and Rosie locked the door behind us. Dad walked around the entire building with the shotgun.

Then he came back and made sure Rosie got into her car safely and then put me back into his car and we all drove away. I don't know why, but I wasn't scared or even shaken up. I guess it was because he was my dad.

Dad brought me back home to 6 Manitou St., he walked me into the house, kissed me and told me he loved me and said, "See ya later," he never said goodbye, it was always "See ya later," always! And before he pulled away he would beep his horn twice. I always took that as an extra I Love You!

Anthony "Guv" Guarnieri Comes to Rochester

There were reports that Anthony Guarnieri was coming to Rochester before my father and the others were falsely convicted on murder charges. He was not seen and there were no reports of Guarnieri in Rochester while the men were in prison. But once the fabricated trial testimony and evidence were discovered and the men were released from prison, Anthony Guarnieri did indeed return to Rochester on the orders of crime boss Russell Bufalino.

It was sometime during the months of February and March of 1978.

Guarnieri came to Rochester several times to meet with my father. They were private meetings, just the two of them. Guarnieri had been sent to Rochester by Russell Bufalino as a peacemaker and had no intention of trying to take over the Rochester Mafia or leave the "misfits" in charge of anything.

Anthony "Guv" Guarnieri

Attempts on Sammy's Life

During February and April 1978, five unsuccessful attempts to kill Gingello by means of explosives were made. Salvatore "Sammy G' Gingello was known to frequent the Blue Gardenia Restaurant in Irondequoit, N.Y., which was located in a busy shopping center.

B-Team members hid remotely controlled devices in snowbanks surrounding the restaurant with the intention of detonating the bombs as Gingello approached the premises. On two occasions Gingello failed to show up and on the other occasion the device failed to detonate.

On or about **Feb. 24, 1978**, B-Team members Didio, Vaccaro, Celestino, Barton, and Frassetto devised and attempted to carry out a plan to kill Gingello inside the Blue Gardenia Restaurant.

Frank Frassetto entered the restaurant carrying a remotely controlled pipe bome inside an attaché case. After determining that Gingello was present, Frassetto was to go to the pay phone inside the restaurant to place a call to William "Billy" Barton and advise him that Gingello was present. Frassetto would then proceed to the bar area of the restaurant.

Barton would then place a call to Celestino, Didio and Vaccaro, who were at a pay phone near the shopping plaza and could observe the front of the Blue Gardenia Restaurant. Barton would then advise the other B-Team members that Gingello was in the restaurant and they could prepare to remotely detonate the explosives from the parking lot.

Barton was then to call the Blue Gardenia restaurant and ask for Gingello. Frassetto would then leave the premises as a signal for his cohorts to detonate the device, which was left by the phone booth in the attaché case.

If this plan had been successful, numerous patrons and employees of the restaurant would have been killed or severely injured upon detonation of the device. The plan, however, failed to work because when Frassetto attempted to telephone Barton, he consistently got a busy signal. It was later determined that this was due to Barton having an extended conversation with his girlfriend.

On **March 2, 1978,** the B-team returning to less elaborate plans planted a remotely controlled device in a snowbank in front of the Blue Gardenia Restaurant. Frank Frassetto was in the parking lot of the shopping center, with Dominic "Sonny" Celestino secreted in the trunk of the vehicle with the remote radio signaling device required to detonate the explosives.

A hole had been drilled in the trunk of Frassetto's car so that the antenna for the radio device could be extended outside the vehicle to insure detonation of the device.

Salvatore "Sammy G" Gingello arrived at the Blue Gardenia in a vehicle operated by John Fiorino. Stepping in front of the restaurant, Gingello got out and approached the front door at which time Celestino detonated the explosive device. Due to the manner in which the device was placed, Gingello was blown into the air, but miraculously escaped serious injury. Shrapnel from the device caused damage to the front of the restaurant and adjoining buildings.

(pages 442-443 1978 Senate Hearing)

Gina Gingello also vividly recalled the **March 2, 1978** bombing incident. She said it was the first time her father actually realized that he was not indestructible.

March 2, 1978

On **March 2, 1978**, at 11:30 a.m., there was a ten-inch galvanized steel pipe-bomb placed in a snow bank at the Blue Gardenia's parking lot. It detonated as dad walked up to the building. His nose and the side of his face were scorched in the blast.

He did not want me to see him like that, but as always we talked on the phone every day and every night. It took about ten days before I was able to see him again. He used to tell my mother Janice, "I'm like a cat, I have nine lives." But after that happened, he told her, "I guess I'm not like a cat I only have one life!"

Private Body Guards March, 1978

Dad was released from prison on Jan. 30, 1978. In mid-March of that year we were driving to Bishop Kearney High School to register for school. Undercover police officers were following us and dad made a joke about it, saying, "We have our own personal bodyguards."

Security Surveillance (before dad died)

They (the police) had such close surveillance on my father that one day when they couldn't find him they sat outside of my house on 6 Manitou St. facing Clifford Avenue. My mother and I pulled into the driveway and they were parked right in front of the house in an undercover police car. There were two men in suits, with two rifles in the middle of both leaning on the windshield.

Me, being me, I walked toward the police car as my mother was saying, "No Gina no." I walked up to the car and asked the men what they wanted. The guy in the passenger seat said, "Nothing."

So I told them, "He's not coming today. I just talked to him earlier." Then I walked into the house. Maybe about 15 minutes later they pulled away. But after that I could still see them driving slowly up and down the street. Then they parked at the doctor's office at the corner of Clifford and Manitou Streets, which was the way my father would normally come.

That was the type of surveillance my father had on him for years. So where the hell were they the night he was murdered. Even when I was with my father the police continued their surveillance, to the point that he would often joke about having our own personal bodyguards.

They could sit in front of my home and at the corner of my street every single night, but they were no where to be found on the night my father was murdered? Perhaps it was because the police knew what was going to happen, and those Son's of Bitches let it happen.

To this day, no one and I mean no one has been charged with his murder-despite 40 years of investigating. Why has no one ever been charged?

Old Charge on Gingello is Dismissed

Old charge on Gingello is dismissed

A 3-year-old indictment charging Salvatore "Sammy G" Gingello with criminal possession of stolen property was dismissed in Monroe County Court yesterday because a key witness against Gingello reportedly has said he isn't sure his grand jury testimony in 1975 was correct.

On **March 31, 1978,** a three year old charge of possession of stolen property was dismissed after a key witness against Salvatore Gingello stated that he wasn't sure that his previous grand jury testimony was correct.

The article stated that Gingello was originally indicted on Jan. 16, 1975 and charged with buying a stolen diamond wristwatch from Zeke Zimmerman. (48)

Bank Account

My father didn't believe in bank accounts. But there must have been some reason in the first weeks of **April 1978** that he opened an account. He only put $20 in. That must have been what you needed to start an account.

I found out years later that they started that account when they found the money and his name came up. That's when I realized he must have felt a certain way about what was going on in his life.

I do believe my father thought that Rene, Red and Dick would have done the right thing and provide for his family, the same way he provided for Dick Marino's family when he went to jail. And if things were different he would have provided for Rene and Red's wives, too. But not one of them stepped up to the plate. No class sons of bitches.

That's okay though, I was taught to earn things on my own and pay my own way in life. And I never owed anyone anything just like my father.

April 22, 1978
The Last Time I Saw My Father

On **April 22, 1978,** like usual, dad came driving down Manitou Street and of course there I was, in the street. I forgot who it was that yelled "heads up" to warn me that my dad was coming. All I remember is that instead of me catching the ball, it hit the hood of his car.

I thought that's it I am getting punished for sure now. So I grabbed the ball and threw it back to the kids and then I walked over to the driver's side window. Tommy Taylor was in the passenger seat. I kissed dad, blew a kiss to Tommy, and I waited to hear my punishment. But there was no punishment.

We talked for a few minutes and he told me, "Dad will be back tomorrow and you and I are going to play some catch together." Wow, that never happened before. I was so excited, just him and me playing catch.

But as we all know, tomorrow never came. Instead a phone call did. A phone call that changed the rest of my life. I don't remember what time in the morning it was. It think it was my aunt waking me up, telling me she had to talk to my mother. By the look on her face I could tell that it was not good news, but the words that came out of her mouth were unbelievable! Your father died. He was blown up in his car.

I don't remember getting out of bed, washing up, or even getting dressed. But I did because the next thing I remember was holding my baseball mitt and ball and throwing the ball against the stoop and playing catch-by myself.

In between looking down the street and waiting for him to drive down it, people started coming over. People giving me sad hugs and kissing me, I just wasn't having it. He's fine I kept on thinking. He'll be here. Finally I could not take hearing "I'm Sorry" anymore. I ran across Clifford Avenue with my mitt and ball to Common Terrace and sat on the wood fence, for I don't know how long.

Across the street two old men started talking and I heard one of them say, "Did you hear that they got him? They killed Sammy G." Of course me being me, I jumped off of the fence and began arguing with them and telling them they were wrong. One of them said to me, "Kid you don't know what you're talking about, he's dead!"

"NO HE'S NOT. MY FATHER'S NOT DEAD. You don't know what you're talking about," I responded, grief stricken. The look on their faces! Right at that moment a white Lincoln Continental came pulling down the street. It was Mr. Sofia, Patty's dad. He raised his voice and said, "Everyone's been looking for you, get in the car." And I did. He did not say another word. He just held me tight and just let me finally cry.

On the left is the Sofia family. From left to right, are Joann, Patty, Anthony (Tony), Mr Sofia, Stephen (Steve), and Terry. In 1978 Patty Sofia was my best friend. (Photo from July 5, 2013)

147

Saint Philip Neri School Girls Softball Team

My dad sponsored the girls softball team when I played for Saint Philip Neri School. He bought all of the baseball equipment at Zambito Sporting Goods store on Culver Road. He never got to see us play. Not even one game. He had passed before we started.

But when we were shopping for the baseball equipment dad was like a kid in a candy store. He swung every bat they had. He wanted to make sure that we had a variety of weights for the bats. He bought us balls, a catcher's mask, bases, and of course a large duffel bag to carry everything in. We were in that store for over an hour.

Being in the Eighth Grade we had a year book at St. Philip Neri School. The kids in my class all wanted to dedicate the year-book to my dad because the majority of the kids knew him personally. The rest knew him as just a nice man. But some of the parents wouldn't stand for it. Just knowing that my classmates cared enough to even suggest it was enough for me.

So when my father died my classmates wanted to attend the funeral. The kids all had permission from their parents to come. It was so beautiful. They walked in to the middle of the floor at Profetta Funeral Home and lined up behind each other. There was a nun on both sides of the row of children. They all knelt down at the same time and said a prayer.

Everyone else in the room stepped aside as soon as they realized what was going on. Of course my closest friend and classmate, Patty Sofia, was by my side. Peter Dellefave, Chucky Mastrodonato, Johnny Ricketts, and Michael Cobb were also there. Peter, Michael, Johnny and Leon were the Altar Boys and Patty was the Altar Girl at my dad's Mass.

Even though we went to St. Philip Neri School, for Patty, Michael, Johnny and myself, our church was St. Francis Xavier.

April 24, 1973

Dear Parents,

Since Gina Gingello is a member of the Eighth Grade class, we shall be attending the wake and funeral for her father.

If you do not wish your child to attend either the wake or the funeral, please indicate below.

The wake is at Profetta's Funeral Home (Goodman and Bay St.) and the funeral Mass is at 9:00 a.m. on Thursday at St. Francis Xavier Church.

Please sign and return slip below by tomorrow.

Grade 8
ST. PHILIP NERI SCHOOL

My son/daughter _____
(child's name)

has my permission to attend:

_____ Wake - Tuesday at 2:30 p.m.

_____ Funeral - Thursday at 9:00 a.m.

_____ Neither wake nor funeral

_____ I can drive for the funeral on Thursday.
        (leave school at 8:30 a.m.)

PARENT SIGNATURE: _____

Sam Gingello sponsored the girl's baseball team at St. Philip Neri School, where his daughter Gina attended. When Sam passed away the entire eighth grade class was allowed to attend both his wake and his funeral. Above is the "permission slip" that was passed out to all of Gina Gingello's schoolmates in the Eighth Grade at St. Philip Neri School.

149

Sympathy Card

This sympathy card was sent to Gina Gingello from the Eighth Grade class at St. Philip Neri School, and signed by most of the class.

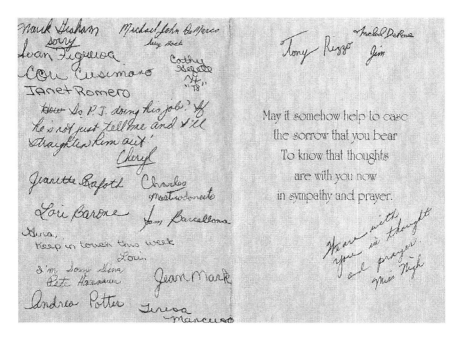

Fulfilling His Purpose in Life

In my eyes my father had fulfilled his final reason, purpose, and job on earth. My father had a usual day. He talked to his mother, Grandma G. He drove around town seeimg people including Tommy Marotta, and he made semi plans for that night. The one and only thing that was different this day was he had never met his first great-niece, Christina (Tina) Lynn Gingello-Lana.

So he made it a point to go to his sister's house to finally meet Tina. The reason that he never met her before was she lived in California with her mom and dad. She was 10 months old when my father finally met Christina (Tina) Gingello - Lana.

When he pulled down Manitou Street that was the first thing out of his mouth. His eyes were sparkling. The smile on his face was priceless. And the tone in his voice describing her to me was so loving. He kept on repeating how beautiful she is.

As for his sister, Aunt Mickey's recollections of their day went like this. He held her in his arms so tight. He kept on telling her (Tina) how beautiful she was. He introduced himself to her (Tina). "I'm your Uncle Sam and I'm so happy to meet you," he said, while giving the baby little kisses around her little head and face.

I am a true believer in we were all put on this Earth for a reason, purpose, and a job to do. I also believe that once we have completed that, we are called back home to God Almighty in Jesus Christ his Son. I believe after my father met his great niece he had fulfilled his reason, purpose, and job that God intended for him to do. And then it was time for him to go back home.

AMEN

The following is what the United States Senate concluded happened on **April 23, 1978**, the day Salvatore Gingello died.

ORGANIZED CRIME AND THE USE OF VIOLENCE HEARINGS BEFORE THE PERMANENT SUBCOMMITTEE ON INVESTIGATIONS OF THE COMMITTEE ON GOVERNMENTAL AFFAIRS UNITED STATES SENATE
NINETY-SIXTH CONGRESS
SECOND SESSION
MAY 2 AND 5, 1980

"In the early morning hours of **April 23, 1978**, B-team members Thomas Didio, Angelo Vaccaro, Dominic "Sonny" Celestino, and Frank Frassetto placed a remote control device under Salvatore "Sammy G" Gingello's vehicle, which was parked in a lot in front of Ben's Café Society on Main and Stillson Streets in Rochester, N.Y.

At approximately 2:30 a.m., Gingello and his two A-team bodyguards, Thomas Taylor and Thomas Torpey, returned to the vehicle. As Gingello and his associates entered the vehicle the device was remotely detonated and the explosion completely destroyed the vehicle and caused damage to the surrounding vehicles and business locations.

The force of the explosion amputated Gingello's right leg and severed the left leg at the thigh. Within 20 minutes Gingello died at Genesee Hospital as a result of injuries suffered in the explosion. Thomas Taylor and Thomas Torpey suffered less extensive injuries.

The following day, Dominic "Sonny" Celestino was reputed to have stated that if he had placed the bomb properly, he would have, **"gotten all three of those bastards."**

(page 444)

152

April 23, 1978 Sam was Killed

Salvatore "Sammy G" Gingello was killed on **April 23, 1978**. He was 38 years old. He would have been 39 years old on Oct. 24, 1978. (49)

Saint Francis Xavier Church, pictured at left, is where Mass for Salvatore Gingello was held following his death. The picture is the way it looks today.

Tom Marotta Stood by The Gingello's, as Always

Tom Marotta was the only person that stuck by me and my family. He stayed by my side during the funeral, fighting off reporters who were trying to get into the church. My father had to stay in the Chapel at Holy Sepulchre because the mausoleum wasn't finished being built.

It was madness just driving from Profetta Funeral Parlor on Goodman and Bay Streets to St. Francis Xavier Church. The streets were lined with crowds of people. There were even people on rooftops filming the procession.

The church was packed. It was unreal. One photographer managed to make his way in and up to where the organist was and he took a photograph of my father's casket, below. When I first saw that photo I was so pissed off. But now I am glad I have it.

Family and friends of Salvatore "Sammy G." Gingello gather as his coffin is carried into the chapel at Holy Sepulchre Cemetery. Gingello died in a car bombing on East Main Street on April 23, 1978. STAFF FILE PHOTO

So after we left the church we went to the Chapel at Holy Sepulchre Cemetery. The Chapel was not very big so as many people as could fit inside did, and the rest stayed outside. There were rows and rows of people until finally they were forced to close the gates leading into the cemetery.

Holy Sepulchre Cemetery

D&C photo by Talis Bergmanis

Shut out of the cemetery, bystanders watch from a distance.

Bystanders were watching Sam Gingello's funeral procession from a distance after the gates to the cemetery were closed.

After the service, "blue eyes" himself, Thomas Marotta, made me wait in the Chapel while he moved people along to leave. He told me to wait and he would be right back. I found myself alone in the Chapel, directly in front of my father's casket.

How did this happen? How did he end up like this? There we were, just him and me. And even though I didn't think I had another tear left inside of me, I did. Still in my hand was Tom Marotta's handkerchief that he had placed there earlier to wipe away my tears.

The Chapel became cooler inside after all the people left and it seemed to be getting a little dark. Then suddenly the door opened and the light was shining through and standing there was Tom Marotta. It was like I was frozen to the seat. I knew I had to leave but how could I leave him there all alone?

Tom walked up to me and the look in his eyes was as sad as mine. He put his hand out and said, "It's time to go." I took his hand and both of us at the same time took our free hand and placed a kiss in it and put it on the casket. Then we walked out together.

The crowd had dispersed and there was just a few people left. We waited until the Chapel was locked up and secured. As we pulled out they closed the large Rod iron cemetery gates behind us. I was upset that he was left alone. But he wasn't alone, he was with God and was back home.

Once the mausoleum was finished being built we had to go witness him being put in it. Tom, of course, stood with us, Grandma and Grandpa Gingello, Aunt Mickey, other Gingello's and myself. The rest, Joey Tiraborelli, Dick (Flubb) Fabrizi and some others stood with my father's unfaithful fiancé. So we watched as they put him into the wall and then closed it up. It was sealed with a plaque that had his name on it. But some idiot used the wrong initial for his middle name.

The plaque reads Salvatore F. Gingello. My father's birth name is Salvatore Angelo Gingello. The "F" was for Frank, but that was his confirmation name not his birth name.

Sam Gingello's middle name was Angelo (A) as seen on Gina's Birth Certificate, left.

Later, I heard Father Golden caught some flack for allowing "Sammy G's" funeral mass to be held at St. Francis Xavier as my family wished. Thank You Father Golden for abiding by my families wishes and for not refusing to have the Mass.

Fiancé Gets Plank Road Home

When my dad was in prison his fiancé at the time never made any payments on the house. So, by the time he came home from prison, 14 months later, he was in jeopardy of losing his Plank Road home. So in order to save the house he quick deeded it into his fiancé's name, and after that the house was hers.

After his death she (fiancé) had a private auction and sold all of my father's belongings. The only thing she gave me was a broken baseball trophy, a cubed lighter with the picture missing, and other scraps of things. The lighter doubled as a picture holder, which originally held a picture of my dad and his brother Jim Jr. pretending to box, but even that was gone. Joey Tiraborrelli brought me the stuff in a brown paper bag.

Before that happened my cousin, my aunt and myself broke into the house through the front window. My cousin and I were the ones who went through the window and into the house. It was daytime, but the house was dark. I made my way into my dad's bedroom, and in the closet I found some pictures of my dad and I took one of his hats.

Before Breaking Into the House

Diane Marino came to my home at 6 Manitou St. We sat in the kitchen and she asked me what I wanted. I told her I wanted the ring my dad was wearing when he died. She apparently figured she could get away with lying to a 14-year-old and she told me the ring he was wearing that night was fake.

I knew that my father had two sets of rings. He had the real ones and the fake ones. But that didn't matter to me. I just wanted to have the ring that he was wearing when he died. Diane even tried to dissuade me by telling me that the ring was all covered in blood. But that did not matter to me either I told her. She was finally forced to tell me the truth. They gave my father's ring to John Fiorino and he had already put it in another setting.

What right did anyone, and I mean anyone, have to do whatever they wanted with my father's belongings! But they did, so I broke into his house.

So at 14-years-old my dad was taken from me. His home, too, and all his belongings, right down to the ring on his finger when he died, all were taken away from me. The only thing I had left from my father was his last name. So his name was passed on to my children and now my grandchildren. My father's name lives on and nobody can ever take that from me, NOBODY!

I heard that Joey Tiraborrelli had taken most of my father's clothes along with my father's fiancé. My father loved and cared for Joey, and after everything my father did for him that was the way he showed his respect.

Mafia Chiefs
Plan to Quit

<u>*Police told*</u>

Mafia chiefs plan to quit

By NANCY MONAGHAN
D&C Staff Writer

The two leaders of the Rochester Mafia have told law enforcement investigators they plan to sever their ties with organized crime in this city, one investigator said yesterday.

Police investigating Sunday's gangland slaying of Salvatore "Sammy G" Gingello talked to both Rene J. Piccarreto and Samuel "Red" Russotti. Russotti told police he plans to leave town, and Piccarreto, who now lives in Yucca Valley, Calif., said he plans to stay out of town, one investigator said.

ing, police said. As of now, "the trail (to Gingello's killers) is cold," one investigator said.

By late yesterday three men whom police want to interview had not been located, an investigator said. They are Angelo Vaccaro, Thomas Didio, and Dominick "Sonny" Celestino, who police have identified as being aligned with the insurgent faction of the mob.

A fourth man police said they hadn't located by Sunday night had been interviewed by police early Sunday morning. He is Rosario Chirico.

Vaccaro, Didio and Celestino have not been seen for three weeks by any

April 25, 1978 Democrat and Chronicle

Mafia Chiefs
Plan to Quit

The day after Sam was murdered, police investigators spoke to both Samuel Red Russotti and Rene J. Piccarreto, the "Boss" and the "Consigliore" of the Rochester Mafia. Both men claimed that they intended to sever their ties to organized crime.

Piccarreto was already living in Yucca Valley, California and stated he had no intention of returning to Rochester. The Boss, Samuel "Red" Russotti, said he planned on moving to Florida and retiring. (75)

The newspaper article above appeared in the Rochester, N.Y. evening newspaper, The Times Union. The article is partially reproduced below.

Sammy G. - 'A Soft Touch'

"A Hollywood casting director would have found Sammy Gingello perfect for the role of a 1930's gangster. He was dark and handsome. His real name was Salvatore, but he affected the nickname "Sammy G." His car, until recently, was a Rolls Royce. His suits were flashy, often plaid, with a continental cut tucked at the waist to show off his physique.

He even had a touch of charity that movie audiences would have demanded. "He was a soft touch," an acquaintance said. "If you needed a couple hundred to tide you over, the chances are that he would take it out of his pocket and not mention paying it back."

And, despite the fact that informers said he was the Underboss of the Rochester Mafia, Gingello had no felony convictions until Nov. 10, 1976 when he and others were convicted of the murder of Vincent "Jimmy The Hammer" Massaro. The murder convictions were overturned when Detective William Marks admitted to fabricating evidence at the trial."

Richard Tuttle

**Richard Tuttle,
Newspaper reporter.**

Gina was only 14-years-old when her father died. Sammy's death hit Gina hard. Emotionally distraught over the loss of her father, Gina also had to face the almost daily barrage of newspaper articles about her dad. Most of the coverage centered around Sammy's ties to organized crime.

Intending to set the record straight, Gina contacted Richard Tuttle, a local reporter from the Democrat and Chronicle newspaper, who had been running articles about her father.

Richard Tuttle was touched by Gina's story and eventually befriended her. In fairness to Gina and to his readers, Tuttle allowed Gina to tell her side of the story about her father, the side that the news never told. Father, friend, provider and confidant, Sammy was all those things to Gina.

A month after Sam's death, the Democrat and Chronicle ran a story written by Gina. It was a love story about and to her father. Finally the world was going to see the other side of Sam Gingello, the only side that Gina ever knew.

Mr. And Mrs. Richard Tuttle, the columnist that printed Gina's story. Mr. Tuttle had become friends with Gina and attended her graduation ceremonies at Saint Philip Neri. The photo was taken in the parking lot.

Above is the newspaper article that Richard Tuttle had written in the Democrat and Chronicle newspaper about attending Gina Gingello's Graduation ceremony. It is also reprinted here.

Just recently I went to Gina Gingello's graduation from St. Philip Neri School. We had started out with an adversarial relationship. I'd written about her father in this column. He was killed in the mob struggle for control of the rackets. She disagreed with what I had said.

We talked about it several times and out of those talks came her story about her father, which was picked up by Gannett News Service and the Associated Press and reprinted around the country.

Gina had asked Joyce and me to come to her graduation but she hadn't spotted us in the crowd and wasn't sure we had made it.

After the Mass, Gina came out of the school building still in her gold graduation robe. She stopped at the end of the sidewalk and looked around expectantly, smiling.

"Gina," I called and went over to her. She threw her arms around my neck and kissed me.

"Thank you," she said.

(Richard Tuttle is managing editor
of the Democrat and Chronicle)

A Love Story
by Gina Gingello

By Gina Gingello, a love story

Gina Gingello

On May 21, 1978, the Democrat and Chronicle ran Gina's "Love story" about her dad. The above article is reproduced below in its entirety.

Gina Gingello is 14 years old. She goes to St. Philip Neri School. She called me last night because of my letter to the Reader column of Sunday, May 14. I had explained this newspaper's coverage of the funeral of Salvatore "Sammy G" Gingello, Gina's father. Someone killed him by exploding a bomb under his car and I described him as a power in the underworld of Rochester.

Gina Gingello definitely did not like what I said.

I explained then and in later meetings with Gina and her mother that I would not argue with the daughter of a man who had just been killed.

"I would not change your opinion of your father if I could," I told Gina. "I am interested though in your memories of your dad and I think our readers would like to share those memories. Write a story for the paper. I'll run it." She did. Here It is.

-Richard B. Tuttle,
Managing Editor

Salvatore "Sammy G" Gingello
My Dad
By GINA GINGELLO

"I'm writing this editorial about my dad because I want you to know how he really was. My dad was a good, loving father and friend to me. We had the best father-daughter relationship anyone could have.

He was also a good provider. Like when he worked on construction when I was a baby, my mom would sit me out in the driveway so that when he came home every day he would see me and say, "That's who I'm working 10 hours a day for."

My birthdays were special to my father and he always had his own special message written on the cake for me. For instance, my very first birthday cake said, "To My Little Princess." My mom told me about this.

For my second birthday, he had "To My Little Love" put on the cake. My cakes always had to have either a doll with a frilly dress or ballerinas on the icing as decoration.

Even when he was in prison, he had roses sent to me for my birthday. When I was in kindergarten I learned the story about the gingerbread man. My father was so proud of me he made me tell that story to everyone!

He came to my dancing recitals too. He was always there and if I spotted him in the audience, I would stop dancing and wave to him and he'd laugh and tease me about it later.

When I was four or five years old, just him and me would sit in the living room on my little chairs and have dinner at the little card table.

For Christmas, he always put up and decorated the Christmas tree. The first Christmas tree he bought me was a silver tree, which I still have and will always keep.

One thing I'd like everyone to know; my dad and I were always close. He always made me feel like I was a grown up and not a little girl.

When he was in prison he once wrote to me and said how proud he was of me because I was trying to get him moved from Comstock Prison back to Auburn Prison so I could see him more. He said, "Daddy realizes now that you're not a little girl anymore, but you'll always be Daddy's little girl."

For my last report card, I started to slack off because it was getting close to the end of the year. The subject I wasn't doing so good in was math and I couldn't understand how he could be so good in math and I wasn't that hot. But he didn't punish me. We just sat down and talked it over.

I've always been a tomboy. I liked playing baseball and football out in the street when I was seven or eight years old. Sometimes when he would come over to see me there I would be playing ball in the street. He'd tell me to go into the house and put on a dress. But when he left, I'd change back and go outside and start playing again.

But I wasn't as smart as I thought because sometimes he would just drive right around the corner and come back and catch me.

One thing I admired about my dad was that he was always helping someone. Even when he was in prison, he was trying to help other people.

He always made you feel that if you needed anything he was always there, like recently he sponsored the girls baseball team at my school, St. Philip Neri. He bought us new equipment and he was going to buy us shirts and hats.

My father did not live a violent life. The reason you would think he led a violent life is because of what you have read in the paper and heard on the news. My dad, no matter what he did, was put in the paper. And everything that was put in the paper was later proven wrong. He wasn't found guilty of anything.

For the Massaro murder trial my dad was put in prison for 15 months. After he left the city I wasn't able to see him for two months. When I was able to see him I had to ride 10 hours up and back to see him only once a week for five hours.

When my dad was in prison, he lost 15 months of his life and I lost 15 months being without him.

I've always been very open with my dad. I'd even talk to him about things most girls would talk to their mother about. He was always someone to turn to and talk with. And during the time in my life when he was in prison I was very confused. I was mixed up. I couldn't understand why they were doing this to him; why they had to take him away from me.

But the day came as he said it would:

"The ways are many

But the end is one.

I'll see you soon because

I'll be home soon."

When he did come home, he answered all my questions and solved all my problems. When I'd ask for his advice he'd always give me the best answer he knew how. Like when someone would say something to me about him and I'd get upset, he'd always say, "You have to respect everyone's opinion, no matter who or what it is about. You can dislike someone but never hate anyone."

That's what my dad taught me.

After he was out of prison, we were riding in the car one day and he kept looking in the rearview mirror. I asked him what he was doing and he laughed. He said he had his own private bodyguard. I think he recognized an undercover policeman following us.

My dad used to take me to the Blue Gardenia Restaurant for dinner, but then someone exploded a bomb in the parking lot. I read about it and asked him if that was meant for him and he said he didn't know. But we didn't go there anymore.

We were riding in the car one day and one of dad's friends was sitting in the front seat and I was in the back. His friend said that I could get in the front, too. My dad said no. he wanted me in the back seat.

He made me realize after what happened at the Blue Gardenia that there were people who liked him and people who didn't. My dad was respected by a lot of people and disliked by few. The people who didn't know him were the ones who didn't like or care for him. But the people who did know him loved and respected him.

At my dad's funeral many people told me, "Your Father was a good man and helped everyone he could and don't forget that."

I hope you realize now that my dad wasn't as bad as the paper and the news programs made him out to be. He was a loving and caring father, son, brother, uncle, cousin and friend. I loved him." (50)

**Gina Gingello,
age 14**

Gina Gingello's Story Becomes National News

Daddy's Little Girl Remembers

By GINA GINGELLO

I'm writing this editorial about my dad because I would like you to know how he really was.

My dad was a good, loving father and a friend to me. We had the best father-daughter relationship anyone could have.

He was also a good provider. Like when he worked on construction when I was a baby, my mom would sit me out in the driveway so that when he came home every day he would see me and say, "That's who I'm working 10 hours a day for."

My birthdays were special to my father and he always had his own special message written on the cake for me. For instance, my very first birthday cake said, "To My Little Princess." My mom told me about this.

For my second birthday, he had "To My Little Love" put on the cake. For my third birthday, he had "Daddy's Little Girl!" put on the cake.

My cakes always had to have either a doll with a frilly dress or ballerinas on the icing as decoration.

Even when he was in prison, he had roses sent to me for my birthday.

When I started kindergarten, I learned the story about the gingerbread man. My father was so proud of me that he made me tell that story to everyone!

He came to my dancing recitals, too. He was always there and if I spotted him in the audience, I would stop dancing to wave to him and he's laugh and tease me about it later.

...

WHEN I WAS about 4 or 5 years old, just him and me would sit in the living room on my little chairs and have dinner at the little card table.

For Christmas, he always put up and decorated the Christmas tree. The first Christmas tree he bought me was a sil-

Gina Gingello is 14 years old. She goes to St. Philip Neri School in Rochester N.Y. She carries her last week because of evil Letter to the Reader column in the May 14 issue of the Rochester Democrat & Chronicle. I had expressed this on reader's concerns of the funeral of Salvatore "Sammy G" Gingello, her father. Someone killed him April 23 by setting a bomb under his car. Her dad was described as a power in the underworld of Rochester. He was convicted, along with others, of murdering another mob figure, Jimmy (The Hammer) Massaro, but he and others, after slightly more than a year in prison, were released when some defectives from the sheriff's department admitted to having fabricated some evidence. Gina Gingello said her dad was a good one. I explained that and in later meetings with Gina and her mother that I would not argue with the daughter of a man who had just been killed. "I would not change your opinion of your father if I could," I told Gina. "I am interested, though, in your memories of your dad and I three our readers would like to share these memories. Write a story for the paper. I'll run it." She did. Here it is.

RICHARD B. TUTTLE,
Rochester D&C
Managing Editor

ver tree which I still have and will always keep.

One thing I'd like everyone to know: my dad and I were always close. He always made me feel like I was a grownup and not a little girl.

When he was in prison, he once wrote to me and said how proud he was of me because I was trying to get him moved from Comstock Prison back to Auburn Prison so I could see him more. He said, "Daddy realizes now that you're not a little girl anymore, but you'll always be Daddy's little girl."

For my last report card, I started to slack off because it was getting close to the end of the year. The subject I wasn't doing so good in was math and I couldn't understand how he could be so good in math and I wasn't that hot. But he didn't punish me. We just sat down and talked it over.

I've always been a tomboy. I liked playing baseball and football out in the

(Continued on Page 2)

Gina Gingello: A letter to the editor.
Associated Press Photo

Mob daughter: My dad was good and I loved him

ROCHESTER (AP) — Gina Gingello, 11, telephoned the Rochester Democrat & Chronicle recently to complain about the newspaper's story on her father's funeral. Someone had killed Sammy Gingello by exploding a bomb under his car and the newspaper said her dad had been a power in the Rochester underworld.

Richard B. Tuttle, manager editor, offered to print the girl's thoughts on her dad. Here are excerpts from her letter:

"I'm writing this editorial about my dad because I would like you to know how he really was.

"My dad was a good, lov-

buy us shirts and hats.

"My father did not live a violent life. The reason you would think he led a violent life is because of what you have read in the paper and heard on the news. My dad —no matter what he did— was put in the paper. And everything that was put in the paper was later proven wrong. He wasn't found guilty of anything.

...mouths.

to see him, I had to ride 10 hours up and back to see him only once a week for five hours. . . .

[Editor's Note: Gingello was convicted of murder in connection with the 1973 slaying of Vincent (Jim my the Hammer) Massaro but

A Daughter's Memories of Her Slain Dad

By Gina Gingello

I'm writing this editorial about my dad because I would like you to know how he really was.

My dad was a good, loving father and a friend to me. We had the best father-daughter relationship anyone could have.

He was also a good provider. Like when he worked on construction when I was a baby, my mom would sit me out in the driveway so that when he came home every day he would see me and say, "That's who I'm working 10 hours a day for."

My birthdays were special to my father and he always had his own special message written on the cake for me. For instance, my very first birthday cake said, "To My Little Princess." My mom told me about this.

For my second birthday, he had "To My Little Love" put on the cake. For my

(Continued on Page 2)

The story that Gina Gingello wrote for the Democrat and Chronicle about her father was so popular that it soon became national news as her father's death and her story was carried in newspapers across the country.

Losing and Finding My Purpose in Life

After dad died I tried to kill myself three times. I had a razor and attempted three times to slice my wrist. The scars are faded but never the pain I still feel deep in my soul. At that time I could not imagine life without my dad. He was my everything. I no longer had any reason to live.

I was so mad at God. Why would he have taken my father from me? My heart, my soul, my being. I had no meaning without my dad. I was just a shell of a person. I first had accepted that I lost him when he was sentenced to 25 years to life in prison. But then he came back to me on Jan. 30, 1978 when he was released from prison. But it would only be for a short while. And then I had to lose him all over again.

Why, why would God be so cruel to me? What had I done so bad to deserve having everything taken away from me, not only again, but this time forever? But God had other plans for me. I gave birth to three amazing children.

Angelo Salvatore Gingello-Conti was named after my father. My father's name is Salvatore Angelo Gingello, my son Nico Deano Gingello Tortatice, whose middle name was after his uncle Deano Tortatice and Santina Marie Gingello Tortatice. We thought Santina was going to be a boy so we originally named her Santino and planned on calling him Sonny after my dad. But when we found out it was a girl we feminized the name to Santina.

Then at the age of 14, Rocky's oldest daughter, Christina, who lived in Florida with her mother, came into our lives, becoming our oldest child, completing our family. She, too, is amazing. We are very blessed. Rocky and I have four great kids and seven healthy beautiful grandchildren and hopefully more to come.

Our children chose to pass on their family names to their children so that our grandchildren's last names are Gingello and Gingello-Tortatice. The reason why I kept my father's last name and passed it on to my children was because everything else was taken from me, everything except for my last name. It was the only thing that no one could ever take from me!

*Not all of Gina's grandchildren appear in this book due to concerns expressed by the parents. One of the parents being Gina's son Angelo.

"On **June 18, 1978** local police were doing surveillance of both A-team and B-team members. A vehicle containing Dominic Celestino and Frank Frassetto attempted to elude police. During the ensuing chase the men threw several weapons out the window. Police recovered a M-1 sawed off carbine and charged both Celestino and Frassetto with illegal weapons possession.

As a result of Frassetto's arrest, ATF special agents initiated a neighborhood canvas of Frassetto's residence (Lida Lane in Greece, N.Y.). Frassetto's neighbors told investigators bizarre stories of unusual activities in and around the Frassetto residence. Carloads of men were seen entering the house at all hours of the day and night.

A mysterious "Wise Potato Chip" truck would appear at the residence from time to time, and men wearing brown gloves would remove and place items into the truck. Men apparently not related to the Frassetto's would live at the residence for periods of time.

Investigators subsequently identified the Frassetto residence of as a focal point of B-team activity. Numerous meetings were held there and most of the explosive devices were manufactured in the basement."

(page 445-446 of the May 2 and May 5, 1980 Senate Hearing)

"On **June 28, 1978,** ATF agents were surveilling the Wise Potato Chip truck and they observed Anthony Chirico and Rodney Starkweather remove a beer cooler from the truck. It contained a large quantity of explosives, blasting caps, timing mechanisms, batteries, remote radio transmitting devices, and other miscellaneous component parts used to construct explosive devices."

(page 446 of the May 2 and May 5, 1980 Senate Hearing)

On **June 28, 1978,** Rodney Starkweather and Anthony Chirico were charged with possession of explosives after ATF agents witnessed them removing a beer cooler full of the devices.

On **July 6, 1978**, the leader of the insurgent B-team, Thomas DiDio, was machine gunned to death at the 45 Motel in Victor , N.Y. A Thompson sub machine gun and two sawed off shotguns were recovered a short distance from the murder scene.

On **July 30, 1978,** B-Team member Rodney Starkweather was ambushed by two men wearing ski masks. He was shot three times but lived.

On **Nov. 16, 1978,** five Rochester-area men were arraigned on charges stemming from the Mafia-style bombings of local gambling establishments. The men were identified as Rodney J. Starkweather; Rosario F. Chirico, Chirico's son; Anthony Chirico; Francesco Frassetto; and Frassetto's wife, Betty Frassetto. The exact nature of the charges was not known at the time. (76)

Threats Concerning the Lawsuit

$50 million in lawsuits

By NANCY MONAGHAN
D&C Staff Writer

Monroe County faces more than $50 million in lawsuits brought by men who claim they were maliciously prosecuted by overzealous Monroe County sheriff's detectives and a former assistant district attorney.

Seven major lawsuits are pending against the county and many of its law enforcement officials, but it will be several months before any are decided.

Six of the lawsuits involve the illfated prosecution of the gangland slaying of Vincent "Jimmy" Massaro. The seventh was filed by former city Fire Chief Joseph Nalore, who was twice prosecuted and acquitted on arson conspiracy charges and is suing for $8 million.

Because of complicated insurance coverage, it is unclear what effect the lawsuits will have on county taxpayers if the county loses. But a total loss on all the suits could add up to $30 per $1,000 of assessed property value on every taxpayer's bill.

The Massaro trial lawsuits were filed after a detective admitted he and others lied in grand juries and at trials to imprison the men charged with Massaro's murder. All the convictions were immediately overturned and five men were released from custody after serving a year of their sentences.

The men, and the amount of damages they claim, are: Samuel "Red" Russotti, $10 million (and $2 million for his wife, Ida); Rene J. Piccarreto, $10 million (and $2 million for his wife, Rita); Eugene DeFrancesco, $10 million; Thomas Marotta, $6 million (and $2 million for his wife, Mary); Richard Marino, "in excess of $10,000" (he claimed $4 million in his preliminary notice of the lawsuit); and Samuel Campanella, "in excess of $10,000."

Campanella wasn't convicted of the Massaro murder. Although he was accused, the charges against him were dropped midway through the trial for lack of evidence.

Among the law enforcement officials named as defendants in one or more of the lawsuits are: Sheriff William M Lombard; Family Court Judge Raymond E. Cornelius, a former assistant district attorney who prosecuted the Massaro case; former Chief of Detectives William C. Mahoney; former Detectives William P. Marks and Anthony Malsegna and suspended Detective Lt. John Kennerson.

Yesterday Mahoney and Kennerson were indicted for conspiracy to fabricate the key police testimony at the Massaro trial. Marks admitted the conspiracy on Jan. 30, 1978, and pleaded guilty to a civil rights violation at that time. His sentencing has been postponed pending the federal grand jury's investigation of the sheriff's department.

There was more than $50 Million dollars worth of lawsuits filed against the City of Rochester for malicious and wrongful prosecution of the Massaro case.

Well everyone gathered up their attorneys to sue the City of Rochester for being wrongly accused of crimes that they did not commit and for false imprisonment. There was $50 Million dollars worth of lawsuits against the city of Rochester. This was about a year after my father's death. We obtained the services of attorney Richard Miller.

Mr. Miller came to my home on 6 Manitou St. and sat at the kitchen table. He filled out some paperwork and informed me that since I was considered a minor and my father was not married at the time, I needed to have an adult represent my interests. So who better than my father's parents, and they were more than willing to do so.

Mr. Miller made it clear that we did not have to pay him a retainer fee to initiate his services. He said that his fee would come from the lawsuit money. So we thought Mr. Miller was filling out all of the proper paperwork and handling everything that needed to be handled.

Then one day my grandmother came to my house on Manitou Street. Grandma Gingello told my mother and me that she had received a phone call. She would never say whom it was from and she took that information to her grave. She was told to drop the lawsuit that was filed on behalf of the Gingello children.

The caller told her specifically, "You've already lost two sons do you want to lose another?" My father was murdered and my uncle died at the age of 30 from stomach cancer. But the message was clear.

The look in my grandmother's eyes said that she was scared, hurt, and sad. She was crying hysterically and kept saying how sorry she was and she hoped that we would understand. She was intimidated into withdrawing the lawsuit. What choice did I have? My grandmother had already been through so much and now she feared for the life of her last remaining son, Tony. I don't know for sure if she even told Grandpa Gingello who it was that threatened their son Tony's life. It was never spoken about ever again. (77)

8 Indicted in Mob Killings

On **April 12, 1979**, eight men were indicted in a 14-count indictment for a series of "bombings and killings" related to the Mob war. They were specifically charged with conspiracy, obstruction of justice, and illegal possession of weapons and explosives. The indictment charged the men with attempting to kill Sammy Gingello at least twice, on Feb. 6, 1978 and March 2, 1978. But curiously no one was specifically charged with the murder of Salvatore Gingello.

Two men, previously undisclosed, were among the eight men. They were Stanley Valenti and William B. Barton, a former A-Team member. (83)

2 new names

8 indicted in mob killings

The other six people indicted were Anthony Chirico, Rosario Chirico, Dominic "Sonny" Celestino, Angelo Vaccaro, Francesco Frassetto Jr. and his wife, Betty Frassetto.

The Rochester Mob war has generally been considered as having been started in Jan. of 1978 when the upper echelon of the Mob was released from prison. But according to the indictment the men charged had been "in league with each other" as early as May 1, 1977. At that time they were making plans to bomb gambling parlors and were making the bombs themselves. By October of 1977, Rosario Chirico had already made the remote control device and by December they were attempting to get explosives.

Frank Frassetto Charged with Murder and Attempted Murder

On **June 20, 1979**, Frank Frassetto was specifically charged with **"murder and attempted murder"** in connection with the death of Mafia Underboss, Salvatore Gingello.

Frassetto is charged with conspiracy to commit arson, racketeering, and possession of explosives, as well as murder and attempted murder in connection with the death of former Mafia underboss Salvatore "Sammy G" Gingello.

Before the grand jury two months ago, Mrs. Frassetto was asked to reveal her husband's whereabouts when a bomb exploded under Gingello's car.

"Was Frank Frassetto with you on April 23, 1978 at approximately 2:30 in the morning?" She refused to answer.

There were other questions Mrs. Frassetto refused to answer for the grand jury, and Wisner read those in court. "Did Mr. Valenti come. . .to your house and visit you. . .on a Sunday

June 20, 1979
Democrat and Chronicle

Frassetto was also charged with conspiracy to commit arson, racketeering and possession of explosives. According to the newspaper, "all" the men named in the federal indictment were accused of bombing gambling parlors and **killing Sammy Gingello.**

The other men charged were Sonny Celestino, Anthony Chirico, Rodney Starkweather, Angelo Vaccaro, and Stanley Valenti. (78)

*Despite these charges, the murder of
Salvatore Gingello is still considered to be a cold case.

Mental Exam Asked for Alleged Mob Bomber

In **October 1979,** Frank Frassetto, one of the B-Team members facing federal weapons, racketeering and conspiracy charges, claimed that he was temporarily insane as the result of a 1974 or 1975 car accident. He planned to use that excuse in court as a defense, and his attorney presented the federal prosecutor with a Dr.'s note stating that Frassetto was a paranoid schizophrenic under the care of Dr. Christopher Keets, a psychiatrist at Strong Memorial Hospital. (79)

Mental exam asked for alleged mob bomber

The U.S. government is requesting a court-ordered mental examination for Franceso Frassetto Jr., an alleged mob bomber who claims he was temporarily insane after a car accident.

Gregory A. Baldwin, lawyer for the Organized Crime Strike Force has asked U.S. District Court Judge Harold P. Burke to order a mental examination for Frassetto.

Frassetto, 30, of 190 Lida Lane, Greece, has filed notice that he plans to use insanity as a partial defense against federal weapons, racketeering and conspiracy charges in connection with last year's mob war.

A struggle for control of the rackets involved a series of bombings, shootings and two murders, including that of mob underboss Salvatore "Sammy G" Gingello.

According to court documents, Frassetto presented the federal prosecutor with a doctor's letter stating that Frassetto is a paranoid schizophrenic. Papers say the letter was written by Dr. Christopher Keets, a psychiatrist at Strong Memorial Hospital.

Frassetto apparently told federal prosecutors he was involved in an accident in which his automobile was struck from the rear sometime in 1974 or 1975. Frassetto told prosecutors he later saw a psychiatrist and that he was a patient at Strong Memorial Hospital's R-Wing (psychiatric) last winter.

Baldwin has asked for the mental examination to be conducted at government expense to determine whether Frassetto is fit to proceed with trial.

James Bates Testifies about Frank Frassetto

James Bates

On **Jan. 21, 1980,** James Bates, a former B Team member turned informant, testified at the trial of Dominic "Sonny" Celestino, Frank Frassetto and the other men charged with conspiracy, weapons violations, racketeering, and obstruction of justice following the death of Salvatore Gingello and the confiscation of the motherload of explosives. Bates was a former employee of Frassetto working together at Dad's Farm Market on Mt. Read Boulevard and Maiden Lane.

Bates testified that he went to Frank Frassetto's home on Lida Lane in Greece in an attempt to borrow a delivery truck, but was told by Frassetto that the truck was not available. The reason it wasn't available was because it was parked across the street from Frassetto's Farm Market and was being used to store explosives. But Bates also testified that later that night Frassetto called him back and said he needed guns. So Bates said he delivered a sawed off shotgun to Frassetto at his Greece home that same evening.

Bates testified that Frank Frassetto told him that he and some other men were taking over and that Frassetto would be the "number two man" in Rochester. Bates said he was sent out more than once to follow Sammy Gingello. He was with Frassetto, Celestino, Anthony Chirico, and Rodney Starkweather when a bomb was placed at The Social Club of Monroe at 1266 Clifford Ave. It exploded on June 8, 1978, destroying the place.

Bates said he did other tasks for Frank Frassetto as well that included hiding explosives and providing him with guns after his mid-June arrest. Bates testified that he met Frank Frassetto at the Holiday Inn in Greece the day after his arrest, and that Frank was being visited by Stanley Valenti. (80)

Pair given 30 years in Sammy G Killing

Frassetto

R. Chirico

Barton

A. Chirico

Vaccaro

Celestino

All six men were convicted on **Jan. 30, 1980**, after a four week trial, of a bombing conspiracy that resulted in the death of Salvatore "Sammy G" Gingello.

U.S. District Court Judge Lloyd F. MacMahon scolded each man prior to sentencing, calling them all a menace to society. He sentenced each man to varying amounts of time according to the degree of their involvement. Dominic "Sonny" Celestino and Frank Frassetto received the longest terms of 30 years each.

Prior to sentencing, Judge Mac-Mahon reserved his strongest remarks for Frank Frassetto and Sonny Celestino. To Frassetto, he said: (81)

"You are a monster...with cold bloodedness, without mercy that can only be described as callous greed. I am going to take you out of society for a good, long time."

To Dominic "Sonny" Celestino, he said:

"You exposed innocent citizens to being blown to bits with one of these bombs. You showed no mercy and the court has no mercy for you. You are rotten to the core."

Chapter 6:

The Prosecution of
The Conspirators

William 'Back Room Bill' Mahoney
Convicted of Conspiracy
to Violate the Civil Rights of 16 Individuals

In 1974, Chief of Detectives William Mahoney master-minded an elaborate scheme to net him some members of organized crime. The plot involved setting up low level Mafia affiliates (boosters and fences) and then threatening them with jail time in order to get them to rat out some of their customers, who were members of the Rochester Mafia.

It was a good plot:
A super cop busts
the mob, until . .

Later the plot progressed into fabricating evidence and false testimony in order to gain convictions on Mob guys for various crimes discovered through informant testimony. The false testimony (from police) and fake evidence was necessary to corroborate informant testimony.

Conspiracy Plot Unravels

The conspiracy plot first began to unravel in **August of 1976** when Al DeCanzio notified federal authorities with accusations of widespread corruption within the sheriff's department. DeCanzio was a special prisoner in the Monroe County Jail after his murder conviction due to his status as an informant.

His special prisoner status gave him access to police files. For 12 months DeCanzio secretly copied information from detectives' files and sent it to federal authorities. Then finally, in **September of 1977,** the U.S. Department of Justice approved a civil rights investigation into the sheriff's department based on information provided by DeCanzio and detective Lawrence T. Ronayne.

The major allegation against the sheriff's department was that Mahoney, Kennerson, and William Marks fabricated evidence that was used to convict six reputed Mafia leaders of murder.

On **Sept. 15, 1977** sheriff's detective Lawrence T. Ronayne stopped at FBI headquarters and said he knew for a fact detectives had fabricated evidence, because he was asked to give false testimony at Richard Marino's trial. (82)

Soon the headlines would look like this.

'Backroom Bill'
Mahoney: From top cop to prison

On **Sept. 22, 1977,** Chief of Detectives William Mahoney was suspended from his job and charged with official misconduct for having two police informants operate heavy equipment at his home while they were supposed to be in jail. Mahoney eventually pleaded guilty and was sentenced to one year in jail. (51)

Back Room Bill

On **Oct. 4, 1977**, a federal grand jury was empaneled. Four months later William Marks sat in a courtroom telling his story.
[82]

On **Jan. 31, 1978,** Detective Marks admits surveillance notes were fabricated.

On **April 23, 1978,** Sam Gingello was killed by car bomb. William Mahoney was reportedly seen across the street from Gingello's car at a restaurant just moments before the explosion.

On **April 12, 1979,** William Mahoney and three others were indicted on five counts of violating the civil rights of 14 individuals by maliciously prosecuting those individuals with fabricated evidence, including 11 alleged members of the Rochester Mafia.

Mahoney's conspiracy against the mobsters unraveled when Billy Marks, a former sheriff's detective, admitted to lying to the grand jury and at the trials of the men accused of the Massaro murder. The indictment filed against the former prosecutors and police officers was very serious indeed. It listed 150 overt acts that showed a pattern of detectives making up evidence and bringing phony charges in order to force men to cooperate.

Specifically the indictment accused Assistant District Attorney Patrick Brophy of withholding evidence and tailoring witness testimony to his instructions in order to gain convictions. Brophy is said to have helped six witnesses in two separate trials "shade their testimony," starting with Zeke Zimmerman. He gave false statements himself and misled both the judge and the jury in the Al DeCanzio murder trial. He also gave false testimony at that trial.

Assistant District Attorney Raymond Cornelius was accused of ignoring several warnings that his prosecutions were tainted. He was accused of promising one man immunity and then prosecuting him anyway. He allowed three witnesses to lie at the Massaro murder trial and he threatened DeCanzio not to contradict detective Kennerson's testimony at a grand jury proceeding. (52)

William Mahoney

By **December of 1980,** Mahoney was on trial. He was one of four men who stood accused of violating the civil rights of 16 individuals by fabricating evidence, and purposely using fabricated evidence at their trials in order to gain convictions.

Two of the men charged, Raymond E. Cornelius and Patrick J. Brophy, were former Monroe County Assistant District Attorneys. Mahoney and former detective Joseph Robortella were police officers.

The charges stemmed from a police investigation called "Operation Step Up." Police were putting the squeeze on low level boosters and fences, hoping that they would rat out higher-ups with the Mob guys being the real target, since they were known to purchase stolen goods. William Mahoney was accused of masterminding the plot.

Mahoney, not surprisingly, denied any wrongdoing and placed the blame squarely with two overzealous detectives from the sheriff's department, John Kennerson and Billy Marks. Mahoney claimed Kennerson came to his office on June 16, 1975 with a folder, and informed him that he had surveillance notes from Nov. 23, 1973, the night of the Massaro murder.

But John Kennerson testified that he and Billy Marks were specifically requested to fabricate the surveillance notes by William Mahoney, right after Assistant District Attorney Cornelius suggested that the detectives "come up with something." (55)

Informant Angelo Monachino and Detective John Kennerson

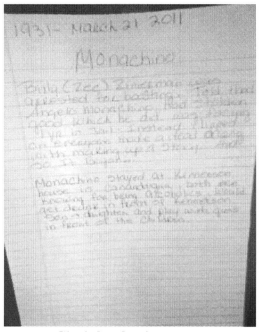

Gina's hand written notes concerning Angelo Monachino.

Prior to detective John Kennerson coming clean about his involvement in fabricating evidence at the Massaro trial he was personally in charge of guarding Mafia informant Angelo Monachino.

While in police custody, Angelo Monachino stayed at Detective John Kennerson's home in Canandaigua.

Both men were known for being alcoholics. It was rumored that they would get drunk together at Kennerson's house and play with loaded guns in front of Kennerson's son and daughter.

This information was given to Gina by a personal friend who wished to remain anonymous.

John E. Kennerson - Sheriff's Lieutenant
Enters Federal Witness Protection Program

John E. Kennerson

John E. Kennerson had been suspended from his job in 1978. He, too, was indicted on April 12, 1979 when a federal grand jury formally accused the sheriff's lieutenant of a massive conspiracy to violate the civil rights of 16 men. Kennerson maintained his innocence for several months until January of 1980, when he entered into the Federal Witness Protection Program.

Kennerson was only the second police officer in the history of the country to enter into the program, which was designed primarily to protect Mafia informers.

On **Feb. 14, 1980,** Kennerson pleaded guilty to a felony conspiracy charge. He admitted to fabricating crucial evidence (making up surveillance notes) along with William Marks, which were then used to convict Massaro murder defendants.

Kennerson
The man who blew the whistle on case

John E. Kennerson was originally indicted for civil rights violations with the other cops. But he pleaded guilty and then entered into the Federal Witness Protection Program.

Kennerson said that Chief of Detectives William Mahoney asked him to make up the surveillance after Raymond E. Cornelius suggested it. Kennerson's false testimony was used to convict Richard Marino of the Massaro murder in 1976. Kennerson even recommended to the judge that Marino be sent to prison for life. (56)

Assistant District Attorneys Patrick Brophy and Raymond E. Cornelius , Chief of Detectives William Mahoney, and detective Joseph Robertella were all accused of fabricating evidence and encouraging witnesses to lie.

Zeke Zimmerman testified that Mahoney asked him to do him a favor. The favor was lying at a grand jury hearing, which Zimmermann said he did.

Charles Monachino testified that he agreed to shade his testimony after the former assistant District Attorney requested him to do so.

Francis Pecora testified that Mahoney sent him to Buffalo on a shoplifting spree and threatened him with jail if he did not comply.

Lawrence J. Masters testified that Mahoney held him captive for 18 hours and threatened to hang him with the motor vehicle robbery if he did not "cooperate."

William Mahoney

Mahoney Convicted of Violating Civil Rights

William Mahoney was convicted on **Dec. 21, 1980** of conspiracy to violate the rights of 16 defendants. He was found guilty of helping to make up evidence used to convict six mobsters of the Massaro murder.

Mahoney was sentenced to one year in jail, but served only weeks of that sentence while released pending an appeal. He died less than one year later.

Police Officers Involved in Operation Step-Up Charged with Various Types of Misconduct

John B. Kinnicutt, Monroe County Undersheriff, was suspended for 28 days for receiving two cases of liquor from an informer.

John Kovak, sheriff's detective, pleaded guilty to purchasing a gun from a Mafia informer. He was suspended, then later quit.

Anthony Malsegna, sheriff's detective, guarded Al DeCanzio while he worked at Mahoney's home. He was convicted of perjury for testifying about a stakeout that never happened.

Dennis Marinich, polygraph operator for the sheriff's department, told a grand jury that he altered test results in return for overtime pay and use of a county car.

William Marks, sheriff's detective, admitted to fabricating surveillance notes used to convict Massaro defendants.

Joseph Robortella, sheriff's detective, guarded Al DeCanzio while he ran a bulldozer at Mahoney's home. Indicted for falsifying records and official misconduct, he was sentenced to 30 days in jail and fired from sheriff's department.

John Kennerson, detective lieutenant, lied about conducting a stakeout of the home where the Massaro murder was allegedly plotted. He was indicted and then acquitted of three charges of mishandling money used to buy evidence.

Albert DeCanzio, a convicted murderer, sentenced to 15 years to life in jail, had only served 33 days since his conviction. The rest of the time was spent in county jail, where most days he could be found in Kennerson's office. (58)

Chapter 7:

Life After Sammy, Growing Up Fatherless

June 26, 1982 - Married at 18

I was 18 years old when I got married at St Francis Xavier

Grandpa Gingello (left) and Sam Gingello Jr. (right) walk Gina down the aisle at her wedding.

Church on Bay Street. Saint Francis Xavier was our family church. It was where my mother and father were married, my grandparents before them, where my father's funeral mass was held, and where my son Angelo and I were baptized.

Two weeks before my Grandfather Gingello and my 14 year old little brother, Sam Gingello, walked me down the aisle, I went to the coroner's office with my cousin Tony and my brother Sam. Before I got married I needed to prove to myself that my father was really dead. We had waited there for two hours for two detectives to show up and when they finally arrived, only me and my cousin Tony were allowed in. My brother Sam was underage and had to wait outside.

Once inside the coroner's office I was finally allowed to see the upper half of my father's body. They would not show me his legs. They refused to show me any other pictures. For this reason my mind refused to believe that he was really gone, I still in my heart of hearts wanted to believe that my father was still alive-perhaps in the Witness Protection Program.

When I walked down the aisle, I thought, in my mind, that once I got up to the altar and turned around my father would be standing there because I always felt he was too smart to have let that happen to him, being murdered like that. So, before I made that final step on to the altar I turned around, expecting to see my father saying, "Who's this bum you're marrying?" But it never happened. He was not there. And as I walked the rest of the way up to the altar and Father Golden began the ceremony, I burst out crying. Father Golden was forced to stop the ceremony and wait for me to compose myself. When I finished crying, Father Golden went on with the ceremony.

At the reception I was called away because I had gotten a phone call and I thought for sure, this is my father, he's still alive. But it was not my father, it was Tom Marotta calling me from prison. I was very happy for the phone call from Tom, but very disappointed because I really believed it had to be my father and that he was still alive.

The picture on the left is with my Grandpa Anthony "Musty" Gennell and the picture on the right is with my Grandpa Gingello. I danced with both of them to Daddy's Little Girl.

Every car that passes, any man walking with dark sunglasses I stop and think, could that be him. But I'm a mother of four children and now I'm a Nani of seven beautiful and healthy grandchildren. I would have to hope, if he is alive, he would not be missing out on all this.

I am a grown woman, but unfortunately, emotionally I am stuck at 14 forever. I don't mean to be. I'm sure there are people out there that can understand and realize what happens to a person when something so tragic happens in your life at whatever age. Maybe life does go on, but for me it went on and I'm very blessed, but my heart my soul will forever be 14.

1986

On the left is a basket of flowers that Tom Marotta sent me after I had my first child, Angelo, on Nov. 5, 1986. He is three weeks old in this photo. Tom was in prison and could not be with me then. But he is here for me now and for all my children and grandchildren too, forever.

On Nov. 25, 1986, 20 days after my son was born, Samantha Jo Lana, my god-daughter, was born (pictured on the right). We call her "Sam."

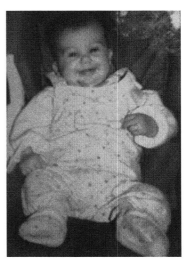

My coats from when I was small had little fur collars and fur around the bottom of the sleeves. I had little fur muffs that you put your hands into and little fur ear muffs too. My nickname from my dad when I was a baby was "Papoose," which is really strange because when my youngest daughter was born she had

190

black hair and reddish-tan skin. She was swaddled up so tightly I looked at her and called her "My little papoose." I had no idea at the time that that was my dad's nickname for me.

It was years later, when one day Tom Marotta called me "The little papoose." I asked him why he would call me that. He said, "Because that's what your dad would call you when you were a baby." So I told him the story about my daughter Santina and how she was my little "Papoose."

It was strange how it made me feel at the time. The next time I looked at my baby girl, who I called my little papoose, it was like he (my dad) was there with me.

Tom Marotta and Gina Gingello Stay Close

Even after Tom Marotta was sent to prison he remained in contact with Gina Gingello, both by mail and by phone. They were very close to each other, like family. Marotta would often give Gina (fatherly) advice, and continued to do so long after he was incarcerated.

The letter below was sent to Gina in **May of 1989** by Thomas Marotta, who was incarcerated at a Terre Haute, Indiana prison at the time.

Hi Sweetheart & Big Boy

This is just a little note to let you know I'm fine, I will call you soon, the holidays make it hard to get to the phone when you want it.

But in the mean time remember everything you hear about me and your dad is all bullshit, you can't believe anything you hear, unless you hear it from me, as far as the newspaper goes don't even buy one, unless you play the horses, or wrap up some fish.

You also know that you should always wipe your own nose, and not let other people clean up your mess, other people don't do a good job.

Angelo, I just loved your picture and I think you better grow up to be a pilot or a doctor, you are very special, and don't think you got like that by chance, your mom is also very special.

Well buddy I'm going now, you stay safe and smile, you have a very pretty smile.

Love
Tommy
P.S. But the end is one!!!

On the left is a photo Gina had of Tom Marotta, taken while he was incarcerated in the early 90s at Milan Michigan Prison. On the top from left to right, are Tom Marotta, Anthony Spero and three others. Bottom left is Johnny USA. ALL NEW YORK GUYS.

How I met Rocky
September 1987

After my cousin's baby shower, my girl cousins and myself went into Norton's pub on Goodman Street to have a couple of cocktails. Who comes walking in but Jerry (Nutsy) Artuso. With him was this gorgeous guy who I thought at first was this guy I went to Bishop Kearney with, but it wasn't, it was Rocco (Rocky) Tortatice. He went up to the bar and immediately sent me over a drink; he was very charming and very attentive to me and introduced himself as only Rocky.

We made plans to meet in the middle of the week for drinks at Norton's. Then I received a phone call from Sam Romano who told me that Rocky was Deano Tortatice's little brother. I met him (Rocky) at Norton's only to tell him I couldn't see him anymore, because as far as I knew his brother was to have supposedly shot Tom Marotta.

John (Flap) Trivingo was in the bar sitting in a booth and called me over and asked me what was going on. I explained to John the conversation I had with Rocky and he said it wasn't true He said that Deano and Rocky were good kids. I told "Flap" when Tom calls me and he tells me it's okay, that's when I will believe Deano had nothing to do with the shooting. And I also told Rocky the same thing.

Within a couple of days I heard from Tom, he called me from prison. I explained to him the situation and how I would never disrespect him in any way. Tommy thanked me and said, "He's a good kid, (Rocky) and his brother Deano had nothing to do with shooting me!" He further went on to explain to me how his own people were trying to frame (Deano) for what they did to him when they brought the kid (Deano) up to the hospital the first time he was shot. Tom said he told them, "No it's not the kid. That's why I was shot the second time," he said.

So once I had permission from Tom Marotta, Rocky and I went out and we have been together ever since. It was as (ROCKY) says, "Love at first sight." Don't get me wrong, there have been many bumps in the road, but we always ended up back with each other. Rocky and I have been through hell and back and we're still both standing and still together going on 34 years.

The Little Man Who was Put on a Shelf: Confronting 'Sonny' Celestino
2000

So one day I received a phone call from my friend Donna Trivigno. Donna was married to John (Flap) Trivigno, who worked for my father. I had known them both since I was a little girl.

Donna and I started working together at the Riverside Convention Center (now known as the Joseph Floreano Rochester Riverside Convention Center) in August of 1985. I worked there for about ten years before I left and Donna worked there until she retired.

Donna Trivingo and Johnny Cocuzzi stand behind Gina Gingello. The picture was taken at the Riverside convention center sometime between 1985 and 1986 when Gina worked there.

My boss, Joseph Floreano, was a pillar of the community, a great person, boss and friend. Anyway, Donna calls me one day, years later, to tell me that "Sonny" Celestino had started working there (RSCC) as a dishwasher. Donna had first called John Cocuzzi to ask him if she should tell me.

At that time I was working across the street at the hotel and in banquets. So all I had to do was walk across the skybridge and go check things out. The good thing was that I still knew a lot of people working there, so no one would question me being in the back service hallway or walking through the kitchen.

Donna knew exactly what time I would show up there because she is the one that looked at the schedule for me to see what time Celestino was working. I walked through, saying hello and talking to everyone. I walked straight back to the kitchen toward the dishwashing machine and I saw him standing there with some lady standing next to him.

As soon as I saw him the rage inside of me became overwhelming. But right at that moment Donna spotted me and she knew me well enough to read the look on my face. So she yells hey "Ging", which was her nickname for me, and walked towards me and started talking to me.

On the third day that I went there scoping him (Sonny Celestino) out, one of the cooks yells out, "Hey Gingello how have you been?" Celestino turned around with a look on his face that said, did I really hear that? Then the cook says, "Hey Gingello and Celestino don't you guys call yourselves Kumamonie Kubaties?" That's when Sonny realized that I was there again, watching him. So he asked me, "Are you here for me?" I told him, "Ya I want to talk to you."

He said, "Lets go to the back loading dock." Since I had previously worked there for ten years I already knew the layout of the building and I knew exactly where all the cameras were. I knew there was one located by the loading dock. But I let him lead the way and acted like I didn't know where I was going. When we arrived at the loading dock I stood with my back against the doors that led into the RRCC. Up in the corner at ceiling level was a camera pointed right directly on me.

Celestino says, "What do you want to talk about?" I asked him, "Was it worth it?" "Worth what," he said. "Was it worth 25 years of your life?" No answer. So then I ask him, "Show me the finger." He said, "What finger?" "The finger that changed my life," I said. I stayed perfectly calm and I did not raise my voice. Anyone who knows me knows that staying calm is not an easy thing for me to do. And I purposely placed my hands in my pants pockets because I always use my hands to express myself.

So then I asked him if he had grandchildren. He said, "Yes." "Do they climb up on your lap," I asked. "Ya," he quietly responded. "Show me the finger that took that away my childhood. Show me the finger that took their grandfather away from my children."

The calmer I was the less calm he became. Finally he said, "Where're the boys," as he moved closer to me. "What boys? I am Sam Gingello's daughter, I don't need any boys. Show me the finger that changed my life forever," I persisted.

He kept getting closer and closer to me. I thought at the time that he was trying to intimidate me, but I found out later that he had cataracts. So this went on for a while. I kept saying show me the finger and talking about me not having a father and my kids not having a grandfather.

Finally he grabbed his head and started yelling, "It wasn't me, It wasn't supposed to happen like that." I looked at this old man's face, his red dishpan hands on his head, he was clearly upset.

I told him, "Now you just told me who it was. My Grandma Gingello used to say every dog has their day. So if it wasn't you then it was Frank (Frassetto)," I said, as I started walking away from him. He came running up behind me saying very loudly, "Are you talking about my friend?" I looked at him and said, "No, you just talked about your friend and now I know for sure from your own mouth," as I walked away down the back corridor and left him standing there holding his head.

Rocky and Tom Marotta were mad at me when they found out what I did. No one knew what I was up to but me. Shortly after that he quit his job at the Convention Center. Later I heard he was in a Veterans Hospital, and according to some staff members he has little to no visitors.

He was later transferred to Hillside Nursing Home on Empire Boulevard. He remained at the nursing home for the remainder of his natural life where rumor has it he died not only blind, but alone. And that in my eyes is called Karma!

2008

Georgia Durante

Georgia Durante wrote a book called "The Company She Keeps." It is an expose on her life and her involvement with mobsters including Sam Gingello. Unfortunately, her memories of Sammy Gingello as recorded in her book did not portray Sam in quite the manner he deserved and those "memories" were rather embellished for her own purposes. Gina Gingello put it this way.

"I spoke to Georgia Durante in person at her book signing when she released her book, titled, "The Company She Keeps." I told Georgia that day that I hoped she did not write anything bad about my father.

This is how Georgia signed my copy of her book, 'To Gina, Your dad was a special person to me and a lot of other people.'

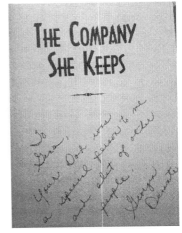

"While waiting in line for Georgia to sign her book 'The Company She Keeps' you had to fill out a sticky note and write what you wanted her to write in your book. I wrote, You better not have said anything bad about my father."

Despite Georgia's nice inscription in my copy of her book, she still said some very unflattering things about my father inside the book.

"I found myself staring into the eyes of a cold-blooded killer." That is what she said about my father, the man who protected her and took care of her since the age of 13.

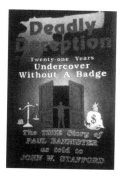

There was even an ex-undercover cop who wrote a book called "Deadly Deception." He described my father as being one of New York's biggest mobsters, not a "cold-blooded killer."

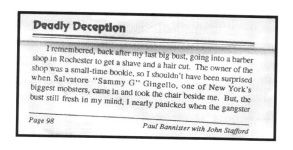

Deadly Deception

I remembered, back after my last big bust, going into a barber shop in Rochester to get a shave and a hair cut. The owner of the shop was a small-time bookie, so I shouldn't have been surprised when Salvatore "Sammy G" Gingello, one of New York's biggest mobsters, came in and took the chair beside me. But, the bust still fresh in my mind, I nearly panicked when the gangster

Page 98

Paul Bannister with John Stafford

Above is the book, "Deadly Deception." To the right is an excerpt from the book.

I told Georgia Durante the story about my own attempted rape and my gratitude towards the boy who saved me because I thought she could relate to it. She knew first hand, having been raped by her own brother-in-law, the trauma of being victimized by men with bad intent. My father had prevented that from happening to her at an even younger age when he rescued her at age of 13.

Georgia just didn't seem to understand why I was so upset about what she wrote in her book. Instead of being forever grateful to my father and giving him the respect and honor he deserved she chose to remember the way she did, repeating her lies to whoever would listen.

Georgia and I shared a similar experience. But there is a difference between us. I had and still have a genuine gratitude and a fond remembrance for the person who saved me from a potential rape while Georgia chose to trade those memories for lies and book sales. I will always be grateful to my hero, Peter Dellafave. Rest in peace Peter. Your name will live on with the honor and respect it deserves. Your memory will never be disrespected the way Georgia disrespected the memory of my father.

Peter Dellefave

I once found myself in a situation with someone. I was 16-years-old and never thought he had any intention of trying to take advantage of me. When he asked me to go upstairs and look at a picture he had drawn of Mickey Mouse, I didn't know that he had locked the bottom door, which was never locked.

He walked into his bedroom and the picture was in there. Being the trusting person I was I followed him in to look at the picture. While looking at the picture and saying what a great job he did he tried to put his arm around me and tried to kiss me.

He was much older than me. I started laughing and said, "What the hell are you doing?" He pushed me onto the bed, but just as he did that someone started pounding on the bottom door, because as I said that door was never locked.

Peter Dellefave

Thank God. It was my "knight in shining armor," Peter Dellefave. Somehow he knew I was in there and that something was not right because the door was locked. Just as he (Peter) was getting ready to kick the door in, my captor went running downstairs and opened it. I was right behind him and I ran out the door.

Peter saw the look on my face, and not asking any questions he grabbed the son-of-a-bitch by the throat and jacked him up. Peter was yelling and swearing at him while choking him. When it reached a point where the fucker could hardly breathe, Peter finally let him go and dropped him on the porch. Peter was someone that loved me, cared for me, and always protected me.

2003
50 Years of Service

In January of 2003, Anthony Gingello celebrated 50 years of service with the City of Rochester, N.Y. For 32 of those years Anthony served as President of the City Employee Union Local 1635. (63)

Anthony Gingello at his office.

2003
Sally Jessy Raphael

Sally Jesse Raphael

Sally Jesse Raphael had a very popular T.V. talk show that aired from Oct. 17, 1983 until May 24, 2002, almost 19 years. Georgia Durante had originally published her book, "The Company She Keeps," in 1983, and appeared on the Sally Jesse Raphael Show at some point after that, telling her web of lies on national TV.

A year after the program aired I was working at the Sheridan 4 Point Hotel in downtown Rochester, where a luncheon was held for a women's organization. And the guest speaker was none other than Ms. Sally Jesse Raphael herself. After the luncheon and the signing of autographs, I asked Ms. Raphael if I could speak to her for a moment. She kindly agreed and we walked away from the crowd to speak privately.

I explained to her who I was and I told her that the guest that she had on her show, Georgia Durante, was a liar who fabricated stories in her book just to sell it. I further explained about my father and the kindness he had shown her and the terrible things she said about him in return.

After I was done speaking, Ms. Raphael brushed my cheek ever so softly, because as much as I tried to contain myself she could clearly see how upset I was. She said to me, "You seem like a very lovely young woman and it is very apparent that you love your father very much. And from what you have told me about him, just know that he sounds like a good man."

She went on to say, "This person Georgia that you are talking about, who you said was on my show last year, apparently did not impress me because I don't remember her."

2010

Two More Gingello Boys Born

Luciano Giorgio Anthony Gingello

Tony Gingello Jr.'s grandson, Luciano Gingello, born Oct. 16, 2010.

Luciano Giorgio Anthony Gingello
Son of Emelia & Salvatore
October 16th, 2010

Gianni Michael Gingello -Tortatice was born on Oct. 12, 2010 to Nico Gingello-Tortatice, Gina's son (below). Gianni is Rocky Tortatice and Gina Gingello's first grandchild. Four days later, on Oct. 16, 2010, Gina's cousin Tony was also blessed with a grandson named Lucian Gingello (above).

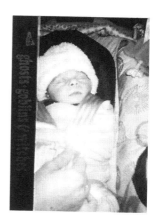

Nico and his newborn son Gianni.

2013

Tommy Marotta with Gianni Gingello, Gina and Rocky's first grandchild, at Webster Park in 2013. Gianni is three.

May 12, 2018
Anthony Gingello Sr. Celebrates 84th Birthday

On **May 12th 2018,** Anthony Gingello Sr. celebrated his 84th birthday with his son, Tony Gingello Jr., daughter Jeanie, and niece Gina Gingello at his home in Chili, N.Y.. Anthony was born on May 12, 1934. He was the first born of his siblings Sam, James Jr., and Michelina. Gina told me, "This was his last birthday, I'm so glad I was there to celebrate with him."

Jeanie brings birthday cake to her father Anthony.

Pictured are Tony Gingello Jr., Anthony Gingello Sr., Gina Gingello and Anthony's daughter, Jeanie.

July 21, 2018
Anthony Gingello Sr. Dies at Age 84

Anthony M. "Tony G" Gingello

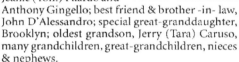

CHILI - May 12, 1934 - July 21, 2018. Anthony is predeceased by his first wife, Rose Gingello; parents, Angela & James; brothers, Salvatore & James. He is survived by his wife, Anita (D'Alessandro) Gingello; children, Jeanie (Tom) Filardo and Anthony Gingello; best friend & brother -in- law, John D'Alessandro; special great-granddaughter, Brooklyn; oldest grandson, Jerry (Tara) Caruso, many grandchildren, great-grandchildren, nieces & nephews.

Anthony served his country during the Korean Conflict with the US Marines. He was the former President of Local #1635 and also the Executive Director of AFSCME. For more information, visit www.bartolomeo.com

Anthony's Life Story will be shared during visitation, 4-8 PM on Wednesday and 4-8 PM on Thursday at the funeral home, 1411 Vintage Lane. His Funeral Mass will be celebrated 9:30am on Friday at St. Theodore's Church, 168 Spencerport Rd. Interment in Holy Sepulchre Cemetery.

Bartolomeo & Perotto
FUNERAL HOME, INC.

On **July 21, 2018,** Anthony M. "Tony G" Gingello passed away. The funeral was a three day funeral, two days at the funeral parlor **July 25 and 26,** then the Service was held at Saint Theodore's Church at 9:30 a.m. on **July 27.** Afterwards there was a beautiful luncheon at the Diplomat Party House. (64)

On the right is the garbage truck that the city brought and put in front of Barolomeo's Funeral Home. It was a gesture that allowed the drivers, that Anthony represented, to pay their respects.

In Memoriam
of
Anthony "Tony" Gingello

In Memoriam

Anthony "Tony" Gingello, former President and Executive Director of Council 66, passed away on July 21, 2018. He was 84 years old. The longtime union leader spent his career with the labor movement.

Gingello served our country as a US Marine in the Korean War. After returning home from the service, he went to work for the City of Rochester in the Water Department. He became active in AFSCME Local 1635 and was elected President of that Local in 1973. In 1984, he became President and Executive Director of Council 66.

Tony had a reputation for blunt talk and for leading the Union with an iron fist. He also negotiated many fair contracts with the City of Rochester during his time as Local President.

We thank him for his many years of service. Rest in peace, brother.

Anthony "Tony" Gingello

I'm Mad at My Father

I'm mad at my father because he didn't allow his body-guards to do their jobs that night. I am mad at my father because he let his guard down and he let his pride get in the way of his safety. I am mad that he left me, only if he had stayed home that night.

Mad But Proud

I'm proud of my father because he stood strong and no one was going to run him out of his city. When the men were released from prison, I heard Rene went to California, Red went to Florida and Dick went to New York City. They all knew something was probably going to happen and they left town. But not my father. He stayed put. There was not a streak of yellow blood in him.

I'm very thankful to Tommy Taylor and Tom Torpey for being there and standing by my father, risking their own lives, not knowing what was going to happen hour by hour. There had already been several attempts on my father's life, but they kept getting in the car with him.

Talking to Tom Taylor after
Tom Torpey Died July 26, 2019

Tommy Taylor at home in January 2020.

After Thomas Torpey passed away on July 26, 2019, I made a phone call to Tommy Taylor. I told him I had a question that I needed answered and there was only two people who could answer it, and one of them was now dead. I also told him that I wasn't a little girl anymore. I have four grown children and six grandchildren.

My question was, What went on the night my father was murdered? Wasn't he supposed to stay home that night? He said, "No we're going out." I heard he got into an argument with his fiancé, but that wasn't true.

When they left the Portland Parkway Manor Apartments where my dad lived, Taylor drove. After returning to the car after their first stop, Taylor went on one side of the car and Torpey went on the other. As they began to kneel down on either side of the car my father asked them what they were doing. Taylor responded, "Checking the car."

From what I have been told my father was more than a little upset. He told them to, "Never do that again." His reasoning (my father's) was if someone was watching them it would be considered a sign of weakness, as if they were scared.

That answer just infuriated me. I raised my voice very loudly at Taylor and told him that was their job. That is what they were paid to do, protect my father. I said, "You guys didn't do your job, why?" Tom Taylor finally convinced me. He said to me, "You don't understand Gina, when your father said something you never questioned him."

I have spoken to Tommy Taylor several times since then and periodically during our conversations he has said to me that it was supposed to have been him that died that night, not my father. He had been driving all night, that night, and should never have given my dad the keys. I know he has survivor's remorse.

What kind of person would I be if I agreed with him that it should have been him and not my dad that died that night. Not the kind of person my father raised. So I told him as I'm telling you, God called my dad home that morning on April 23, 1978. I have to believe that to keep going. He finished his job here on earth and went home to God Almighty.

Thank you Tommy Taylor for answering my calls and my questions, and for the unconditional love you still have for my dad.

The last place they went that evening was Ben's Café on Stillson Street. When they were leaving they were breaking each other's balls and my father asked for the keys to the car. Sam told Taylor, who normally drove, that he was only a laborer and that since he was not a card holding Teamster he couldn't get behind the wheel of a moving vehicle. Sam on the other hand was a Teamster, so he was going to drive. That was their relationship years earlier when they had worked on a construction job together. So Taylor tossed my father the keys.

I once heard a rumor that my father received a phone call and ran out of the bar and jumped in the driver's seat. But that story wasn't true either. The real story, according to Tommy Taylor, was Sammy took the keys and got into the driver's seat. Taylor got into the front passenger seat and Tom Torpey got in the back seat behind Taylor.

My father closed his door and then Taylor and Torpey closed theirs - and it happened. Along with Taylor, Torpey and Tom Marotta, my whole family and myself, all our lives would change forever at that moment.

Suffering From PTSD

In my late 40's and early 50's I began seeing a therapist who diagnosed me as having "Post-Traumatic Stress Disorder" (PTSD). She believes the PTSD started at the age of 14 when my father was murdered.

I eventually found a way to live with it (my father's death), which I credit to the way I was raised, the values I was taught, and the work ethic that was installed in me by my father. As a parent myself I know that no matter what, your children have to come first.

My father was a real person. Just like everyone else he loved, he laughed, and although I never saw it, he even cried, especially when his brother Jimmy passed away at the age of 30 from stomach cancer.

He was the Patriarch of our family. If anyone ever had a problem in the family concerning anything they always ran to dad, even Grandma and Grandpa Gingello. Dad would take care of and provide for all, no matter what. He loved his family unconditionally.

October 2019
My Son Nico's Stag Party

I would like to thank my father's friends; Tom Marotta, Steve Triantafilio, and someone who will remain nameless. They helped me in every aspect of my son's stag party. At first my son did not want one, until he did.

Within two weeks my father's friends stepped up to the plate and helped put it all together. Ticket sales were good. There were raffles, great food, and of course a GREAT card game.

**Nico Gingello-Tortatice,
Tom Marotta, and
Stratos (Steven)
Triantafilou .**

You see, these men are truly my father's friends. My father was not here to give his grandson a stag party but my dad's friends were here and did give Nico his stag party. Stratos (Steven) Triantafilou came to America just before he turned 17 years old in 1967. He told me stories about when he arrived here and how Americans were not very welcoming to him or his family.

But Stratos met Sammy and Tom at the age of 18 on Chestnut Street. Both men treated him with such kindness that to this day he has an unconditional respect and love for the both of them. So a beautiful friendship that started when Steve was 18 years old has continued on into my life. Steve loves telling the stories about when I was a toddler running around the joints. Thank you Steve for always standing by my father and now my children and myself.

A special thank you to the other gentleman that helped out with my son's stag. For reasons I cannot discuss, his name cannot be mentioned but he well deserves a thank you, even if it is anonymously. But he'll know who he is and that it was meant for him.

"IDIOTA"
Frank Frassetto

The very first time I approached Frank Frassetto after my father's death was in **August of 2019**. I went to the Rochester Public Market and walked right up to him at his booth and introduced myself. He acted like we knew each other and said, "Oh, hi honey, how have you been?" I looked at him and replied, "You don't know me." I told him that I wanted to talk to him about my father, but he just kept saying how busy he was and nothing ever came from it.

Frank Frassetto,
as he looks today.

I went to see Frank again on Saturday, **June 13, 2020**. I was told to come back that Thursday but that he goes out of town a lot. On **Thursday, June 18** I had some car trouble so I was unable to make it there. On **Thursday, June 25** at about 8:30 in the morning I went to the public market and was told that he wasn't there. He was out of town and I was directed to where the stand had been moved.

A nice lady asked me if I would like her to call him. I said, "Thank you that would be very nice," and she called him. I could not hear the conversation as she stepped as far away from me as possible, and then she came back and said that he was out of town and asked for my phone number. I gave her my phone number and I've yet to receive a phone call back.

Saturday Nov. 14, 2020 Public Market 10:30 A.M.

I walked up to Frank's son's stand at the Rochester Public Market. Frank was waiting on a customer and he looked over at me and said hello. I pulled my mask down and said, "Do you know who I am?"

He responded and said, "Yes Gina." He was waiting on a customer, and after I was sure that he knew who I was I told him, "Wow Frank you really know how to hurt a girl's feelings, you ask for her number and then you never called." As he started going into how busy he is I had on my phone a picture of him and his family (children and grandchildren) that I found on Facebook.

I showed him the picture in front of his customers as I said, "What right do you have to have this (a family picture) when you took that right away from me?" I think he realized then that I was not going to allow him to blow me off anymore. He called another worker over to take care of the customers on his side of the stand.

He looked at me and said, "Let's talk out here," meaning not in front of the customers. So he walked away and I followed. I started right in on him about the 1982 Senate Hearing Report on Organized Crime that Blair Kenny was kind enough to make a copy of and provide me with.

So with the report in hand I started rattling off a shitload of questions. I told him I now had proof that he stored the materials in his home to make bombs. He started to deny it so I opened up the report and I had his name highlighted along with his wife's name, and how the ATF was watching the Wise Potato Chip truck where the explosives, detonators, and other material to make bombs was taken out of the truck and put into a field not far from the truck. The truck was his truck (Frassetto's). And after it was unloaded the ATF Agents retrieved the containers.

He tried to say he was innocent and that he did his 32 years and never told on anyone. My mind was all over the place. I just kept asking him question after question. I told him how I spoke to Dominick (Sonny) Celestino and how Celestino already fingered him. He smirked at me and made a reference to Celestino's character, like his (Celestino's) word was not credible.

So my next question was, "Why would you get involved

with a bunch of half-wits?" That's when Frank started stumbling over his words. He was not making much sense at all. I asked him, "What did my father ever do to you?"

His answer was, "Nothing, your father was a great man. He helped out a lot of people. I never had anything against him." So then I asked him again, "Why were you involved with those half –wits?" He answered, "Everyone picked a side."

I went on to express my feelings about how I felt about what they did to me by taking my dad, who had only been home (from prison) for two and a half months. About my four children that never knew him along with my seven grandchildren (my father's great grandchildren). I just went off and I wouldn't let him get a word in at that point. When I was finished, this son-of-a-bitch no class asshole looked at me and said that I should go talk to Billy Lupo's kids and see how they feel, implying that my father killed him (Lupo).

That's it. All bets were off. I told him, "You show me something that proves my father had anything to do with Lupo's death. My father died with no charges on him. All previous charges were dropped, and he died an innocent man, unlike you." I was holding the Senate Report on Organized Crime in my hand and I asked him several times to take it and that I could get another copy. But he just kept saying no, and that he was framed by people.

"People? What People?" I said. "The people you chose to be loyal to or were you referring to the ATF that was investigating you?" I just looked at him and said, "Whatever Frank," as I thought to myself now I know for sure. I extended my hand out first to shake his and then the words that were in my head came out of my mouth. "NOW I KNOW FOR SURE," I told him. And I went on to say, "I am writing a book you will be interested in reading."

Thank you to my friend at the Public Market. You know who you are. Love you.

Tony Pecora

Tony Pecora bought the gas station/garage on Bay Street (above) that my family had previously owned. I had heard that he hired some guys to take down the red letters that spelled out G-I-N-G-E-L-L-O, and when they did so he was standing there laughing. So I ran into him (Tony Pecora) at D J's Bar, which is owned by John (Flap) Trivigno, and I told him the story I had heard. He just looked at me with a smug look on his face and said, "Where are the Boys," as he began looking around the bar.

I was there with my Cousin Jimmy's second wife, Sandy. I call her Sandra D. So I proceeded to tell him I don't need any boys, I am Sam Gingello's daughter. I told him to just answer the question. He just stood there with that smug look on his face. I only gave him a moment to answer before I threw my Absolute, with just a splash of Cranberry for color, in his face.

Then I looked at him with a smug look on my face and smiled and said, "Here's the boy you were looking for" and I proceeded to walk out of the bar. As I was walking to the car I turned around to say something to Sandra D. and suddenly realized she wasn't behind me. So after my dramatic exit I had to go back into the bar and get Sandra D.

I found her still standing there staring at Pecora, who was wiping the drink I threw at him off of his face and clothes. I grabbed her and said, "C'mon, let's go." After we got into the car I explained to her that if I throw a drink and leave the bar, then she has to follow me! We laughed our asses off the rest of the night.

Concerning The Medical Examiners Report

On **March 2, 2020**, I went down to the Medical Examiner's office to fill out the paperwork necessary to obtain the information from my father's Medical Examiner's Report. I spoke to a very kind, considerate and compassionate man named Bob Zelby. We spoke briefly on the phone and I told him I would be down there around 3:00 p.m. to get the process of the paperwork going.

When I arrived I was taken into a room and told that I would have to come back on **March 5**. On my way back home Mr. Zelby called me and told me to come right back. So I did. When I got there we went into another room where Mr. Zelby had all the paperwork ready to be signed and notarized. And of course he checked my identification.

As hard as it was for Mr. Zelby to hear and explain all of my unanswered questions it was just as hard for me to hear the answers. But I needed to know the truth concerning my father. When I was 18 years old I went to the Medical Examiner's Office and I waited there for two hours for two detectives to show up because I wanted to see the pictures of my father. They showed me from his waist up to his head, but they would not show me his legs.

So now, nearly 39 years later, my mind would still play tricks on me and tell me that there might still be some possibility that he was still alive, all because I never saw the picture of his legs. So here I have this man, Bob Zelby, answering and explaining to me all of my unanswered questions.

He reassured me that no one could ever get a hold of those photos and that it was his job and the job of the other staff members at the Medical Examiner's Office to protect the dead. It would take a court order for someone to view those pictures. And that someone would have to go before a judge with the request and he would have to have a damn good reason for wanting to see those pictures.

Concerning the Medical Report, he told me, "Once it was in my hands there was nothing anyone could do." I understood exactly what he meant by that. At this time all I have to say about the report is, "God called my father home that day. He completed whatever job God had intended him to do. As for winning and losing, my father did not lose that day and they definitely did not win. They did not win because I am still here and I will fight with my last dying breath to have justice served for my father. Dead or alive they will be held accountable."

My father's murder is a "cold case." But I have called out the Rochester Police Department and the Sheriff's Department to re-open my father's case with the existing evidence they already have, combined with the DNA testing capabilities that they did not have before.

I have spoken to Tommy Taylor, who was in the car the night it exploded killing my father, concerning some details of that evening. I agree with everything that Tommy Taylor has said concerning the night my father was murdered. So for now I've decided to keep the medical report private.

From left, are Gina Gingello, Tom Marotta, and Gina's son Angelo. Marotta is holding a picture of Gina's dad, Sammy G.,
that Gina gave him. Gina said that Tom keeps it (the picture of
Sammy) next to him always. The photo above was taken on
Sept. 20, 2020.

Gary Craig
Democrat & Chronicle
Investigative Reporter

I think it was 2004 when I first spoke with Gina Gingello. That year, as an investigative reporter with the Rochester Democrat and Chronicle, I'd written a major four-part series about a $10.8 million armored car heist that had been partly solved. Even though there were no organized crime figures involved in the robbery, the Rochester Police and FBI were actually keeping an eye on some former "OC" members and those avenues oddly led to arrests in the robbery.

But that's a whole other very long story. As part of my series, I revisited some of Rochester's ample mob history, and that series set me on a path to be the go-to reporter locally about mob history – even though I was not in Rochester for any of it. Of course, the murder of Sammy G was part of the history I revisited in 2004, and that's how I met Gina. Part of our series included a photo of the car that was blown up, killing Sammy. I got a call from Gina, upset that she and her kids had to again revisit the ugly history.

In Gina's remembrance of that call, she was an "asshole" to me, she now says. I don't recall it that way at all. I saw her as a daughter and a mother who was being forced to relive one of her life's most tragic days. If she was angry, so be it. I could understand why. In fact, from then on, whenever I was writing a story that might include mention of her Dad, I would let Gina know, especially if there were to be photos.

We developed a friendship, and an understanding of what each other was doing when those times would arise. I wouldn't eliminate mention of her father's murder – nor, honestly, his crimes – if they were necessary in a story, but I would also not use them gratuitously or sensationally. But I also understood the pain those same stories could cause her, and tried when I could to alert her in advance. She reminded me that there are people affected by our stories, even if I am writing about a notorious mob homicide nearly three decades old.

As reporters, we should always remember this. It might not change the content of our work, but it is a reminder that we should practice sensitivity however we can, even with something as simply providing notice about a forthcoming story. Recently, I wrote a major story questioning whether police were alerted to a possible murder attempt on Sammy G., and pulled back the night he was killed. I spoke with Gina in advance, so she knew what was to come. And, to this day, I still hope to get answers for her. She deserves nothing less.

Gary Craig
Democrat & Chronicle
Investigative Reporter

10-26-20

Separate Families

My father never wanted anyone in his family to be part of the other Family he was involved in. He was very big on school education and he tried hard to install that value in all of us. When my father was growing up school was basically secondary to working and helping out your family, especially if you were a boy.

My father knew the street and he knew the people. But more importantly my father knew how to treat people with kindness and respect. And that is exactly what he received back. I have never been ashamed of who my father was. I was actually very proud of him.

My father would take care of everything on the streets and at home and run a trucking company. He helped people in need. I saw him many times reach into his pocket and give some cash to whoever it was that needed it. You could see the gratitude in people's faces. The look of relief at the realization that they would be able to pay their rent or mortgage or put food on their families tables.

My father was even able to help people by giving them jobs. People like Jerry Artuso, whose nickname was "Nuttie." Jerry was unable to find employment anywhere. Jerry told me many years ago that my father was the only one that was willing to take a chance on him. For that he was forever thankful.

There was another gentleman who knew my dad but wished to remain anonymous so I have to respect that. In his words he told me, "I just kinda keep my stories to myself." But he was willing to share his story with me. This is what he said.

I remember the day your dad came down to the corner (bar) looking for "Flap" (John Trivigno), I called him John because he was my best buddy.

(John owned a bar at the corner of Goodman and Clifford Avenue called DJ's.) He said, "I just bought a lot of trucks and I need drivers." I didn't even know how to drive a truck, but he took me on anyway. I loved him. It was fun working for your dad. He was the best boss a guy could ever have.

My father kept the streets of Rochester, N.Y. safer than any police department or sheriff's department ever could. The police were not even able to control drug trafficking on the streets they patrolled but my father did because he was so violently opposed to drugs.

Anything that happened in the circle stayed in the circle, and no innocent people were ever harmed. I'm not justifying the deaths that occurred before or after my father's death, but I do know that there was something these people did within the "Organization" that warranted the consequences of their actions. None of those people were "innocent."

As for my own father's death, he was murdered by a bunch of misguided misfits. Someone actually preyed upon this group of wannabes and convinced them that they could take over the Rochester Mafia by murdering my father.

I believe it was Stanley Valenti who was behind this bunch of half-wits. He filled their heads with false promises of being somebodies. It was actually reported in the newspapers that an older gentleman would frequently be seen directing the meetings attended by this group when the Mob Wars were just in the planning stages.

In reality, Stanley Valenti was attempting to organize a coup within the organization, on behalf of his brother, in order to restore power back to themselves (Frank and Stan Valenti). They had been dethroned in 1972 as leaders of the organization and my father was one of the three men that dethroned them. It was pure revenge.

I CARRY YOUR HEART WITH ME

◆

i carry your heart with me (i carry it in
my heart) i am never without it (anywhere
i go you go, my dear; and whatever is done
by only me is your doing, my darling)

i fear
no fate (for you are my fate, my sweet) i want
no world (for beautiful you are my world, my true)
and it's you are whatever a moon has always meant
and whatever a sun will always sing is you

here is the deepest secret nobody knows
(here is the root of the root and the bud of the bud
and the sky of the sky of a tree called life; which grows
higher than soul can hope or mind can hide)
and this is the wonder that's keeping the stars apart

i carry your heart (i carry it in my heart)

e.e. cummings

The Memory Pages

In the process of writing this book I asked my father's nieces and nephews and my first cousins if they would like to share a memory about my father, their uncle. Since my father was very close with all of his nieces and nephews, they all said yes and here are their memories.

Memories of Sammy Gingello from His Family

A woman came up to me at his (Sam's) funeral. She told me she flew in from Florida just to pay her respects. She also told me that she would be forever grateful to him for saving her life. It was cold and she was living on the streets. He saw her and gave her his coat, bought her a hot meal, gave her some money, and got her a job as a waitress. That's the kind of caring, compassionate man my Uncle Sam was.

I Love and Miss Him!
Jeanie (Gingello) Filardo

My Uncle Sonny (Sam) was one of the most selfless men I have ever known. He stepped up and took care of his deceased brother's children and we are forever grateful. One of the fondest memories of him was the day he handed me a set of car keys on my sixteenth birthday. Some men have honor, courage and strength, and cannot be duplicated. He is one of them.

Always and Forever,
Angela (Gingello) Lana

Uncle Sam, on my father's deathbed you promised him that you would take care of us kids and you never wavered from that promise. You not only supported us financially and emotionally, but you gave us a loving home where we always felt wanted. You taught me many things that made me the man I am. But mostly you taught me to work hard and that family is everything. I am forever grateful for all you were to me and I hope that I have made you proud.

I Love and Miss You!
James (Jim) Gingello

I'd like to write this about my hero, my Uncle Sam. I had so much fun with him. On one occasion in the middle of the night we went to Don and Bob's in Seabreeze. When we were done eating we headed back to Uncle Sam's house. He lit up a cigarette and offered me one. Of course my first reaction was to say, "I don't smoke." I was 14 years old. As usual Uncle Sam already knew that I did smoke. So I still said no to the cigarette and I told him he would tell my dad. He gave me a smile and chuckled. So I took the cigarette. And later I found out I was the first to smoke in front of him.

Another memory was when he would call me on the weekends and tell me to look out the window and see if anyone was there. I would see headlights and tell him yeah, someone's here.

He would tell me, "I sent a cab for you get in and come over and spend the weekend." With him the weekends would fly by because I had so much fun with him. And it seemed like there was never enough time. I could go on and on but that would be a book in itself.

Thank you Gina for the opportunity to write something. I am glad this book is from my uncle's daughter. So for now Uncle Sam, Rest in Peace. Love, your nephew Tony. You will forever live in my heart.

Always and Forever,
Anthony (Tony) Gingello

The thing I remember the most about my uncle was that he was a classy gentleman, the glue that held our family together. One time at Christmas he gave us kids $100 each all in one dollar bills. I thought I was rich! And I miss him dearly, every day.

Theodore (Teddy) Snacki

I have great memories of my Uncle Sam, who was my mother's brother. When we lost him it was a travesty to our family. He was always about "family first," that's what I admired about him the most.

When I was born he would come over to our house and say to my mom, "Go get the baby." He then would take me and cuddle and lay on the couch with me in his arms. I was his God Child! He always did special things on my birthday and the holidays. He would even take time out of his schedule to pick me up from school at times.

I was lucky enough to be invited to join him, my cousin Gina, Aunt Janice, and Grandma and Grandpa G. to his home in Florida. One day he surprised me by buying me an outfit of my choice off a model at a fashion show. We were going to see Frank Sinatra that evening.

I have nothing but kind loving memories of my uncle to this day. He was a man with a huge heart, a real class act. But most of all I remember the love he had for his family. I have great memories that I hold in my heart.

Mary Ann Snacki-Marshall

I was a baby when my mother moved to California, where her side of the family lived. The only memory I recall is when we came back to Rochester to visit. My Uncle Sam would give me piggyback rides around the house.

I was very young, but I will never forget the love in his eyes and how he would hold me so, so tight.

Love Michelle Gingello-Hall

Conclusion

When Gina and I first spoke about writing a book about her father there were three main goals that she made clear to me that she hoped she could accomplish by writing the book. Her first goal was to "humanize" her father. Sam Gingello was a loving father, son, brother, uncle and much more to many people. But that side of Sam Gingello was seldom, if ever, portrayed by the media. So we included nearly 100 personal family photos and letters in addition to the countless memories provided by family members and friends in an effort to do just that.

Gina's second goal was to write a second, follow up love letter to her father. The first one was written after Sam's death and published in the Democrat and Chronicle in response to all the negative publicity surrounding her father's death. It had been suggested to Gina that she write a follow up letter because it might be therapeutic. So in essence, this book is that second "love letter" to Gina's father and hopefully it has served to accomplish her third goal, which was for this to be sort of a healing process for her while preserving her precious memories of her father, Salvatore "Sammy G" Gingello.

It has been both an honor and a pleasure working with Gina Gingello. She has gone out of her way to provide me with personal information, seek out names, dates and places, interview people, and in general make sure that the information provided here is as accurate as possible. It is my sincere desire that this book serves as a tribute to Salvatore "Sammy G" Gingello, giving him both the honor and respect he deserves.

Blair T. Kenny

P.S. As a direct result of Gina's renewed interest in her father's murder, a "Cold Case" murder investigation has been reopened.

Footnotes

1) Democrat and Chronicle Rochester, New York
09 May 1957, Thu • Page 33 "Police Seize $1,180, Nab 2 as Gamblers"

2) Democrat and Chronicle Rochester, New York
02 Feb 1968, Fri • Page 7 "Stolen Goods Seized in Raid"

3) Democrat and Chronicle Rochester, New York
13 Apr 1979, Fri • Page 13 "Mahoney From Top Cop to Prison"

4) Democrat and Chronicle Rochester, New York
23 Oct 1979, Tue • Page 11 "It was a Good Plot: A super cop busts the mob, Until"

5) Democrat and Chronicle Rochester, New York
17 Oct 1978, Tue • Page 1 "Undersheriff suspended for 28 Days"

6) Democrat and Chronicle Rochester, New York
11 Mar 1976, Thu • Page 17 "Booster Tells of His Life"; Democrat and Chronicle Rochester, New York
27 Feb 1978, Mon • Page 1 "Detective Hid hot Goods Pecora Claims on Tape"

7) Democrat and Chronicle Rochester, New York
07 Jan 1975, Tue • Page 14 "Gingello Turns Himself In, Free on $250 Bail"

8) Democrat and Chronicle Rochester, New York
31 Dec 1974, Tue • Page 7 "Accused Union Chief is Suspended from City Job"; Democrat and Chronicle Rochester, New York
26 Jul 1975, Sat • Page 47 Gingello Loses Union Post After Arrest"

9) Democrat and Chronicle Rochester, New York
16 May 1975, Fri • Page 17 "DeCanzio Nonchalant as Wife Weeps"; Democrat and Chronicle Rochester, New York
14 Mar 1975, Fri • Page 11

10) Democrat and Chronicle Rochester, New York
12 Mar 1978, Sun • Page 29 "Pecora"

Footnotes

11) Oct. 9, 1980 Democrat and Chronicle "Masters says he didn't Rob Office"

12) Democrat and Chronicle Rochester, New York
11 Apr 1975, Fri • Page 21 "Ex Detective courier for Informer"

13) Democrat and Chronicle Rochester, New York
14 Mar 1975, Fri • Page 1 "One freed at Gang Slaying Hearing"

14) Democrat and Chronicle Rochester, New York
04 Jul 1975, Fri • Page 13 "Monachino Tells Court of Our Thing"

15) Democrat and Chronicle Rochester, New York
27 Jun 1975, Fri • Page 9 "Stolen Property Charges dropped against Sammy G Gingello"

16) Democrat and Chronicle Rochester, New York
01 Jul 1975, Tue • Page 1 "Affidavit Signed by Monachino"

17) Democrat and Chronicle Rochester, New York
26 Jul 1975, Sat • Page 47 Gingello Loses Union Post After Arrest"

18) Democrat and Chronicle Rochester, New York
25 Aug 1975, Mon • Page 9 "Gingello Friends eat, drink, give $100,000"

19) Democrat and Chronicle Rochester, New York
08 Sep 1975, Mon • Page 16 "Gingello Finds it a Cold World"

20) Democrat and Chronicle Rochester, New York
16 Apr 1976, Fri • Page 15 "Bias claimed at Hearing'

21) Democrat and Chronicle Rochester, New York
24 Jun 1976, Thu • Page 3 "Marino Guilty of 1973 Murder"

22) Democrat and Chronicle Rochester, New York
27 Aug 1976, Fri • Page 13 "Gingello Elected"

23) Democrat and Chronicle Rochester, New York
21 Oct 1976, Thu • Page 15 "Massaro Trial Jury Sees Site of surveillance"

Footnotes

24) Democrat and Chronicle Rochester, New York
30 Oct 1976, Sat • Page 11 "2nd Witness Reinforces Gingello Defense" ;Democrat and Chronicle Rochester, New York
04 Nov 1976, Thu • Page 24 "Massaro Murder trial in Final Stages"

25) Democrat and Chronicle Rochester, New York
11 Nov 1976, Thu • Page 3 "Profiles of 5 Convicted"; Democrat and Chronicle Rochester, New York
11 Nov 1976, Thu • Page 1 "Five Guilty in Massaro Murder"

26) Democrat and Chronicle Rochester, New York
15 Jan 1977, Sat • Page 1 "Massaro Murderers Get Long Prison Sentences"

27) Democrat and Chronicle Rochester, New York
24 May 1946, Fri • Page 1 "Unions Mobilize to Press Fight ; City gives DPW a Holiday Today" General Strike Mentioned

28) Democrat and Chronicle Rochester, New York
24 May 1946, Fri • Page 39 "tippy goes Right along to Jail"

29) Democrat and Chronicle Rochester, New York
09 Sep 1963, Mon • Page 39 "10 Arrested as Youths Scuffle with Police"

30) Democrat and Chronicle Rochester, New York
01 Oct 1963, Tue • Page 13 "6 in Riot Sentenced to Weekend Jail"

31) Democrat and Chronicle Rochester, New York
02 Feb 1968, Fri • Page 7 Gaming Raid Nets 18

32)Democrat and Chronicle Rochester, New York
01 Jul 1968, Mon • Page 2 "Blow Aimed at Gamblers"

33) Democrat and Chronicle Rochester, New York
08 Sep 1968, Sun • Page 28 "Gambling Raid Nets 31 Arrests"

34) Democrat and Chronicle Rochester, New York
12 Jun 1969, Thu • Page 15 "Man Called in Social Club Probe"

Footnotes

35) Democrat and Chronicle Rochester, New York
03 Sep 1970, Thu • Page 12 "Sammy G. arrested on Speeding Charge"

36) Democrat and Chronicle Rochester, New York
15 Aug 1969, Fri • Page 11 "raid at Bay Street Club Nets Gambling Arrests"

37) Democrat and Chronicle Rochester, New York
24 Oct 1969, Fri • Page 11 "Sammy G and Four Others Convicted"

38)Daily News New York, New York
08 Dec 1969, Mon • Page 6 "says 100G to Pay Bet Debt Was Stolen From Home"

39) Daily News New York, New York
19 Feb 1970, Thu • Page 7 "Rochester Man Linked to Mafia, Slain in Auto"

40) Democrat and Chronicle Rochester, New York
06 Mar 1970, Fri • Page 9 "Gambling Club Shut by Judge.

41) Democrat and Chronicle Rochester, New York
25 Jul 1970, Sat • Page 3 "Raiders Get Defense Quiz"

42) Democrat and Chronicle Rochester, New York
28 Aug 1970, Fri • Page 18 "Sammy G's probation a First"

43) Democrat and Chronicle Rochester, New York
03 Sep 1970, Thu • Page 12 "Sammy G. arrested on Speeding Charge"

44) Democrat and Chronicle Rochester, New York
27 Aug 1971, Fri • Page 13 "Sammy G In Pen, But"

45) Democrat and Chronicle Rochester, New York
16 Nov 1971, Tue • Page 20 "Sammy G Saved from Jail"

46) Democrat and Chronicle Rochester, New York
08 Jul 1972, Sat • Page 14 " Jail Nearer for Sammy G"

47) Democrat and Chronicle Rochester, New York
01 Feb 1978, Wed • Page 23 "Families Feel Relief and Bitterness"

Footnotes

48) Democrat and Chronicle Rochester, New York
01 Apr 1978, Sat • Page 7 "Old Charge on Gingello is Dismissed"

49) Democrat and Chronicle Rochester, New York
13 May 2018, Sun • Page A19 "Funeral at Holy Sepulchre"

50) Democrat and Chronicle Rochester, New York
21 May 1978, Sun • Page 1 "By Gina Gingello, A love story."

51) Democrat and Chronicle Rochester, New York
02 Feb 1979, Fri • Page 4 "It Was A Good Plot Until:"

52) Democrat and Chronicle Rochester, New York
19 Dec 1979, Wed • Page 29 "Indictments"

53) Democrat and Chronicle Rochester, New York
13 Apr 1979, Fri • Page 14 "List of Bad Cops"

54) Democrat and Chronicle Rochester, New York
13 Apr 1979, Fri • Page 13 "Backroom Bill Mahoney from Top Cop to Prison"

55) Democrat and Chronicle Rochester, New York
02 Dec 1980, Tue • Page 12 "Did Mahoney Do Wrong? No Sir"

56) Democrat and Chronicle Rochester, New York
22 Dec 1980, Mon • Page 3 "John E. Kennerson, sheriffs lieutenant"
"Kennerson The Man Who Blew The Whistle on Case"

57) Democrat and Chronicle Rochester, New York
08 Dec 1981, Tue • Page 3 "Ex Monroe Chief of Detectives Dies"

58) Democrat and Chronicle Rochester, New York
20 Oct 1976, Wed • Page 25 DeCanzio/Kennerson

59)Democrat and Chronicle Rochester, New York
26 Apr 2004, Mon • Page 1 "Marotta and wife"

60) Democrat and Chronicle Rochester, New York
28 May 1996, Tue • Page 7 "Strike of 46 defended Local Union Progress"

Footnotes

61) Democrat and Chronicle Rochester, New York
01 Mar 1953, Sun • Page 25 "Chalk Drawing of Mercury Judged Best"

62) Democrat and Chronicle Rochester, New York
08 Sep 1977, Thu • Page 16 "Municipal Union Elects Woman"

63) Democrat and Chronicle Rochester, New York
10 Jan 2003, Fri • Page 39 "50 years of service"

64) Democrat and Chronicle Rochester, New York
24 Jul 2018, Tue • Page A6 Anthony Gingello Sr. obit

65)Democrat and Chronicle Rochester, New York
06 Sep 1986, Sat • Page 9 "City Union Chief Re-Elected"

66) Democrat and Chronicle Rochester, New York
16 Apr 1976, Fri • Page 15 "Bias claimed at Hearing'; Democrat and Chronicle Rochester, New York
02 Aug 1977, Tue • Page 1 "kiler Asks freedom, Protection as a Witness"

67) Democrat and Chronicle Rochester, New York
30 Oct 1977, Sun • Page 1 "Mahoney asked me to Lie About Bulldozer"

68) Democrat and Chronicle Rochester, New York
07 Sep 1959, Mon • Page 30 "Michelina Bride photo"

69) Democrat and Chronicle Rochester, New York
23 Oct 1961, Mon • Page 8 "Anthony Gingello, Ontario Street Garage employee"

70) Democrat and Chronicle Rochester, New York
07 Apr 1962, Sat • Page 23 "2 More Grills Face Charges by SLA on Morals"

71) https://tbrnewsmedia.com/wmho-host-holiday-tribute-show/ "Olivia Newton John"

72) Democrat and Chronicle Rochester, New York
13 Apr 1979, Fri • Page 2 "Kennerson and Mahoney"

Footnotes

73) Democrat and Chronicle Rochester, New York
13 Apr 1979, Fri • Page 5 "Mahoney, Kennerson Charged"
74) Democrat and Chronicle Rochester, New York
13 Apr 1979, Fri • Page 3 "The Monachino's sang for Freedom"
75) Democrat and Chronicle Rochester, New York
25 Apr 1978, Tue • Page 1 "Mafia Chiefs Plan to Quit"
76) Democrat and Chronicle Rochester, New York
16 Nov 1978, Thu • Page 21 "five suspected of Bombings to be arraigned"
77) Democrat and Chronicle Rochester, New York
13 Apr 1979, Fri • Page 3 "$50 Million in Lawsuits"
78) Democrat and Chronicle Rochester, New York
20 Jun 1979, Wed • Page 30 "Jury evidence use disputed in Court"
79) Democrat and Chronicle Rochester, New York
13 Oct 1979, Sat • Page 14 "Mental Exam Asked for Alleged Mob Bomber"
80) Democrat and Chronicle Rochester, New York
06 Mar 1979, Tue • Page 1 "James Bates"; Democrat and Chronicle Rochester, New York
22 Jan 1980, Tue • Page 10 "James bates Testimony"
81) Democrat and Chronicle Rochester, New York
12 Mar 1980, Wed • Page 1 "Pair given 30 years in Sammy G Killing"
82) Democrat and Chronicle Rochester, New York
13 Apr 1979, Fri • Page 2 Mahoney, Kennerson Charged"
83) Democrat and Chronicle Rochester, New York
17 Apr 1979, Tue • Page 3 "8 Indicted in Mob Killings"
84) Democrat and Chronicle Rochester, New York
12 Oct 1969, Sun • Page 42 "Bar Closed-wrong Kind of Shots"
85) Democrat and Chronicle Rochester, New York
01 Feb 1978, Wed • Page 1 "picture of Merberg and Gingello"
86) Democrat and Chronicle Rochester, New York
22 Dec 1980, Mon • Page 2 "Picture of Det. William Marks"
87) Democrat and Chronicle Rochester, New York
26 Dec 1976, Sun • Page 141 "The Muhammed Ali Winning with Humility Award"
88) Democrat and Chronicle Rochester, New York
24 Apr 1971, Sat • Page 11 "Italian Rights Group Pickets FBI"
89) Democrat and Chronicle Rochester, New York
14 May 1971, Fri • Page 1 "Officers of Italian American League Elected"

Other books by the authors:

"The Rochester Mob Wars"

By Blair T. Kenny

© 2017

"The Rochester Mob Wars" is the true story about the rise and fall of the Rochester Mafia. The Rochester Mafia Crime Family boasted over 40 "made" members in its heyday, before internal strife and power struggles led to it's demise by self destruction via murder, shootings, and bombings.

"The Rochester Mob Wars" book is the result of two years of research into organized crime in Rochester, New York. The book is a compilation of newspaper clippings, court documents, and Senate Hearings placed in chronological order detailing the highlights of the Mob's activity over a 40 year period. The 208 page book covers the time period of the 1950's to 1997, when Teamsters Local #398 was put into "Trusteeship" for lifetime affiliation with the Mafia.

Other books by the authors:

"The Black Hand Society of Rochester"

By Blair T. Kenny

© 2019

"The Black Hand Society of Rochester" is the prequel to "The Rochester Mob Wars." Beginning with Italian immigration, the 342 page book uncovers the origins of the Rochester Mafia, which had its roots in the Italian Camorra and their American branch called "The Black Hand." In similar fashion to the Mob Wars book, "The Black Hand Society of Rochester" documents organized criminal activities of Rochester mobsters from 1900-1948. The book comes complete with an index of more than 600 names and eight pages of mobster profiles.

therochestermobwars.com

Other books by the authors:

"Enter The C-Team"

By Blair T. Kenny and Frank A. Aloi

Narrated by Thomas Taylor

© 2020

*

"Enter The C-Team" offers a rare glimpse into the interworking's of the Rochester Mafia as seen through the eyes of Thomas Taylor; friend, driver and bodyguard for Rochester Mafia Underboss Sammy "G" Gingello. Taylor, a former A-Team member, gives a first hand account of fighting on both the A-Team and the C-Team, the third faction in Rochester's Mafia Alphabet Wars. It is a story of bombings, shootings, treachery and murder, highlighting an intense struggle for power. At stake was control of Rochester, N.Y.'s organized Crime Family and all its rackets.

A special thank you goes to Wendy Post, Sample Media Group editor and reporter, former Department of Defense News Writer and Army Veteran residing near Apalachin, N.Y. and originally from Rochester, N.Y.

THANK YOU Wendy for coming through again, at the last minute, with your awesome editing skills.
